Book 1: Dancing in The Fire or Fighting for Life

Series: *Jesus IS ALIVE!*

A True Story about a Living God

Lyubov Oberemok

WESTBOW
P R E S S®
A DIVISION OF THOMAS NELSON
& ZONDERVAN

WestBow Press books may be ordered through booksellers or by contacting:

WestBow Press
A Division of Thomas Nelson & Zondervan
1663 Liberty Drive
Bloomington, IN 47403
www.westbowpress.com
1 (866) 928-1240

Scripture taken from the King James Version of the Bible.

THE HOLY BIBLE, NEW INTERNATIONAL VERSION®, NIV® Copyright © 1973, 1978, 1984, 2011 by Biblica, Inc.® Used by permission. All rights reserved worldwide.

"Scripture quotations are from the ESV® Bible (The Holy Bible, English Standard Version®), copyright © 2001 by Crossway, a publishing ministry of Good News Publishers. Used by permission. All rights reserved."

ISBN: 978-1-9736-7424-5 (sc)
ISBN: 978-1-9736-7423-8 (hc)
ISBN: 978-1-9736-7425-2 (e)

Library of Congress Control Number: 2019913541

Print information available on the last page.

WestBow Press rev. date: 02/10/2020

Being defeated is often a temporary condition.
Giving up is what makes it permanent.
—Marilyn vos Savant

This is a true story about miraculous healing from a rare type of cancer, anxiety attacks, depression, fear and pain, and tears and bitterness by the one and only God. He is always with us—alive and faithful—even when we are not.

This book is about the Living God who is leading ordinary people, his children, step-by-step from grief to victory, from death to life, and from weakness to strength, restoring physical and emotional health.

This book will guide you, give you keys, and teach you how to overcome and help yourself spiritually and emotionally. This is a holistic approach to physical and emotional restoration.

To the Holy Spirit, who inspired and made this book come alive. With deep appreciation for my family and close friends for their support and prayers.

I will extol thee, O Lord; for thou hast lifted me up, and hast not made my foes to rejoice over me.

O Lord my God, I cried unto thee, and thou hast healed me.

O Lord, thou hast brought up my soul from the grave: thou hast kept me alive, that I should not go down to the pit.

For his anger endureth but a moment; in his favor is life: weeping may endure for a night, but joy cometh in the morning.

I cried to thee, O Lord; and unto the Lord I made supplication.

What profit is there in my blood, when I go down to the pit? Shall the dust praise thee? shall it declare thy truth?

Hear, O Lord, and have mercy upon me: Lord, be thou my helper.

Thou hast turned for me my mourning into dancing: thou hast put off my sackcloth, and girded me with gladness;

To the end that my glory may sing praise to thee, and not be silent. O Lord my God, I will give thanks unto thee forever. (Psalm 30:1–12 KJV)

CONTENTS

INTRODUCTION

This is a real story of healing and restoration from a rare form of cancer that the Living God performed in an ordinary Christian family. This woman faced incurable disease, and despite a doctor's prognosis, she decided to trust in God's promises, His Word, and His love.

This story was written to encourage those who are in the middle of the biggest fire, in front of the highest mountain in their lives, who want to be equipped for future battles, and who want to understand and support their loved ones. I want to encourage those who are frustrated, lost, crying, and waiting for an answer to a prayer about a critical situation in life.

This is a story for God's children who worship the Lord, love Him, adore Him, seek Him through their tears daily, and ask Him to respond.

What is it?

Why did this happen to me?

What did I do wrong?

Where are You, my Lord?

When will You answer me and heal me?

This is a story about the faithfulness and love of the one and only Living God. He is always with you—no matter what country you live in, your gender, your age, your income, your education, your marriage status, or your popularity.

Only the Living God will lead you to your victory. Through the fire, He will make you stronger for His kingdom.

The apostle Peter talked about the trials of faith:

> Beloved, think it not strange concerning the fiery trial which is to try you, as though some strange thing happened unto you: But rejoice. (1 Peter 4:12–13 KJV)

As my husband and I were praying, I asked God to give us support in the middle of our needs. After praying, we were just waiting for God's answer in silence. At that time, I was very upset in my heart that we had so many needs.

Suddenly, after our prayer, the Holy Spirit said very optimistically and joyfully to me, "Do you see how many fruits you have?"

I said in my heavy heart, "Really, are these fruits? I meant many needs that I was praying about."

And the Holy Spirit answered me, "Look at your apple tree. Could you eat these small green apples now when their sized like cherries?" The Holy Spirit pointed out the apple tree in our backyard in the early spring season, and they were only the size of cherries. "But when these apples ripen, they will feed many."

His answer led me to seek a divine purpose for my faith. I recognized the trial as an opportunity for a miracle in my life. When I am going through the deepest valleys in my life, God reveals Himself more significantly than before. He is giving me an opportunity to know Him better and be closer to Him than ever before.

> They will be like a tree planted by the water that sends out its roots by the stream. It does not fear when heat comes; its leaves are always green. It has no worries in a year of drought and never fails to bear fruit. (Jeremiah 17:8 NIV)

I wrote the healing words from the scriptures in the Bible on sticky notes and placed them on my kitchen cabinet doors to remind me of His promises for my life. Every time I was in my kitchen, I read them loudly several times. Each time, my voice became stronger and more confident when I claimed God's promises from the Holy Bible:

> But the God of all grace, who hath called us unto his eternal glory by Christ Jesus, after that ye have suffered a while, make you perfect, stablish, strengthen, settle you. (1 Peter 5:10 KJV)

These sticky notes became worn down since I was using them quite a lot, and I changed some of them depending on my prayers, needs, and emotional condition. These words were like life and like oxygen to me every day. I ignored any comments about my kitchen cabinet doors not looking tidy, but most of my family members understood it. I simply could not survive without these promises. These promises brought my thoughts and emotions back to life—in proper order—and adjusted according to the words in the Bible:

> The words that I speak you they are Spirit and they are Life. (John 6:63 KJV)

This promise has always worked for me, and it will work for you. I have good news for you if:

- you have been suddenly diagnosed with a rare form of cancer or another deadly disease
- the doctors do not give you much hope because of your condition or simply do not know how to treat you
- you are suffering from anxiety
- you are alone in the fight for your life and Satan is attacking you by whispering to you about committing suicide.

All things are possible to him that believeth. (Mark 9:23 KJV)

My family and I have been there, and you are holding the right book. Turn to the next page, and this story will lead you in the first steps toward victory with the Lord. David found this victory in his teenage years over Goliath. He was not as mature or as strong as his brothers. You will find the same victory because God never changes His Word.

He sent His Word and healed them and delivered them from the grave. (Psalm 107:20 NIV)

God bless your heart, dear reader.

CHAPTER 1

Warning, Awareness, and Spiritual Vision from God

In the spring of 2013, I was sitting on my porch and found myself thinking that I was totally happy and blessed. I was happy about my relationship with my husband, my lovely garden was blooming, and all my relatives were healthy. What else could a woman wish for?

My husband and I were planning a nice vacation to the Dominican Republic, and after that, I was excited to travel with him to the Middle East for his work. Life was good.

I started to get an unexplainable feeling in my heart that something very big and significant was coming, and I shared my feelings with my husband. I said, "Something huge is coming soon to our lives. I am going to die—or Jesus is coming."

It was a very stupid idea to say what I said: claiming death into my life. I am usually very careful with my words, but in that moment, it was exactly what I felt. I didn't even think about it before I spoke.

It was sunny and warm that spring in Calgary, Alberta. Calgarians are not spoiled with a warm climate. Weather like that makes everyone happy. People smile more than usual when there is sun and it's warm. They expect nothing but positivity in their lives. I was not an exception.

Several days later, our family went to a church service. It was a usual Sunday service at the First Assembly Church in Calgary. I was worshipping with all my heart to our Most High God. He is the only Living God.

I fell in love with God after my mom passed away in 1994 in the former USSR. The divine presence overflowed my heart, and I had a vision. I saw the ocean waves that were forced by a strong wind toward a huge cliff on the shore. It seemed that they had no way to avoid crashing into the cliff. There was no way for the waves to escape. It was a dead end. At that moment, I thought, *I am the ocean, and my children are the waves. Sometimes the wind forces these waves to the cliff. It looks like it is the end, but don't be afraid. I keep your tomorrow in my hands.*

> I am Alpha and Omega, the beginning and the end,
> the first and the last. (Revelation 22:13 KJV)

I asked permission from Pastor Mark to tell other people in the church about this vision from the Holy Spirit. I shared this vision with the church community and assumed the words were for someone else because I did not face any wind in my life and was totally happy, peaceful, and blessed.

> Surely the Lord God will do nothing, but he
> revealeth his secret unto his servants the prophets.
> (Amos 3:7 KJV)

Just a few months later, I was facing the highest mountain in my life. I was suddenly diagnosed with a very rare form of cancer: an adrenal gland tumor that was eight centimeters in diameter. My life changed dramatically in one moment: I had weakness, strong nausea, and depression.

CHAPTER 2

Weird Symptoms and Obscurity

Shortly after several weeks of vacation in the Dominican Republic, we packed our luggage for our trip to Doha, Qatar.

It was June 2013 when my husband and I landed in Doha. It was not my first trip to Doha, but for each trip, I needed time to adapt to the Islamic culture, the Arabian clothes, and the hot climate. The Doha airport was small, and there was a large sign over the border security counters that read "Arabic" to one side and "Other Nations" to the second side.

A few months earlier, I had graduated as a certified nutritional consultant/health coach, and I was excited to begin my own business. I had already lined up a few clients. I was planning a presentation about nutrition and the benefits of a healthy lifestyle, but there was nothing more important than being with my husband and supporting him.

We landed in Doha at night and experienced the same unbearable heat, the same taxis, the same crazy traffic, and the same big and impressive modern buildings. Everyone around me was unusually dressed, and the language was different. Unfortunately, this time, something felt different. After several days, I experienced a very strange feeling of weakness. I knew something was wrong with me.

I was an active person, a wife, and a daughter who took in her dad after her mom's death to take care of him. And I was a mother of two. I was a woman who learned how to make a comfortable home from nothing. A life back home in Ukraine with a military man taught me how to make a welcoming home out of four suitcases, raise two kids with little support from their dad, make delicious meals with any budget, and dress well after restyling old dresses. I never understood people who complained about being bored. I had a long list of chores to entertain myself with each day, but I was rarely able to accomplish everything on it.

I was very healthy, especially when I started to change my lifestyle and diet after completing my nutritional education. The last time I had been in the hospital was when I delivered my daughter, and she was twenty-three years old by then.

This time, not everything was as usual. A couple days later, I began to experience intense nausea. I could not even force myself to eat. I had never been so nauseous and exhausted—not even when I was pregnant. I assumed it was possibly from the not-so-fresh food at the hotel buffet.

When the feeling did not disappear after several days, I decided to fast with water for a couple of days. The hot weather and the feeling of a lack of oxygen in the hotel room where I was staying the entire day, waiting for my husband to come back from work, made me feel even more miserable. A mountain of uncertainty and questions was rising right in front of my eyes. I asked myself, "What is going on with me?" I could not find the answer.

Because of work, my husband was away most of the day. I could hear loud Muslim prayers behind my hotel window several times each day, which made me feel even more spiritually isolated. I was told that the Muslim culture does not allow women to walk alone on the street. They cannot even visit a convenience store a couple of blocks away during the daytime. I felt like I was trapped in a cage as

I sat alone in the hotel room dealing with nausea, unusual weakness, fear, and uncertainty about my future.

It was too much for me to be alone. While I was praying one day, I was interrupted by the loud Muslim prayers that took place several times each day. I could not handle this spiritual isolation by myself anymore, and I ran across the room and grabbed my laptop to find Christian worship music on the Internet.

I found www.christianworship.com, raised my hand in the middle of my hotel room, and gave Him all my fears, pain, and uncertainty. I started to worship the only Living God. He is supernatural and has no limits.

I have been honored and privileged to be in the covenant of love with an obedience to God since 1994. As the tears dropped down my cheeks, I made a decision to cleave to God in this uncertain situation and trust Him for my healing and restoration. I have walked with Him for many years. He has led me by His Holy Spirit daily and has always been faithful and ready to help me—no matter where I am or what happens to me.

It was like an instinct to cleave to the presence of the Holy Spirit in order to survive. I cried to Him and asked Him to help me, to answer my prayer, and to heal me. The presence of God filled the room, and I felt better. However, after a while, the symptoms came back.

I read the Bible and slowly processed every one of His words of healing—words that can never be changed.

> Heaven and earth will pass away, but my words will never pass away. (Matthew 24:35, Luke 21:33, Mark 13:31 KJV)

I was not able to eat anything because of my nausea; each meal was torture for me. I called my friends and kids and asked them to pray for my healing. I was frustrated because I couldn't understand what was going on with me.

CHAPTER 3

Horrible News in the Hamad Hospital

Finally, we decided to go to the hospital to have me checked. The doctors did not find anything wrong. They assumed my symptoms were due to the sudden change in climate or a virus I may have caught during my flight. After urine and blood tests, they released me with a couple of prescriptions for antibiotics.

After several days, my symptoms remained unchanged. A taxi drove my husband and me from the hotel to Hamad General Hospital in Doha. It was a huge building with granite floors, a high-ceilinged lobby, shops, indoor palms, and cozy leather couches. It reminded me of a prestigious five-star hotel. Everyone around me was wearing long robe-like clothes per Arabic traditions. It made me feel isolated even before I noticed that the language was different. It was quite a different experience compared to when I moved from Ukraine to Canada.

After a while, my husband and I found our way to the emergency room. A female doctor gave me an x-tray, checked my temperature, and sent me back to the hotel with more prescribed pills.

Quite a few days later, my symptoms still had not changed. My husband and I went outside where the hot air—as if from an oven—hit us again. It reminded me of a time when I cooked a turkey to celebrate Thanksgiving. Turkeys, my family, celebrations, my home, and Canada were so far away now and in a different time zone. We got into a taxi, and it brought us back to the same hospital. This time, the two doctors from the emergency room thought my symptoms were due to dehydration and heatstroke.

I was really scared. I tried to find a shelter to hide from the sudden blows that had struck my life and transformed me from a confident woman to someone suffering from deep fear, grief, weakness, and depression. It was so sudden, like a severe thunderstorm in the middle of a sunny day, and the symptoms interrupted my whole life. They changed me from a strong Christian woman and a daughter of the Only Living God to a weak person who needed help physically, emotionally, and spiritually. This happened even though I had experienced the presence of God before, enjoyed sharing Jesus and the Holy Spirit, and encouraged others. I found myself in a situation where I was the one who needed help getting back up and being strong again.

I asked the doctor if my husband could stay with me in the cubicle, and the doctor said that it would be fine. I was trying to find support and strength in my husband, and I held his hand tightly in the hospital bed with an IV in my arm. After a while, both doctors, who were originally from India and showed me compassion, were by my side. They tried to calm me down and show me support. Surprisingly, after the IV with water, my nausea disappeared. They let us go back to the hotel with a new prescription for pills.

My son, Andrew, his wife, and my daughter, Alexandra, were praying for me, and they were relieved when we were told that I experienced nausea due to dehydration. Unfortunately, the nausea and all the other symptoms came right back again—even though I was taking all my prescribed pills. My condition became worse, and I became weaker. I could not eat at all because of the nausea. At that point, I was only drinking water and receiving holy water from the Lord when I worshipped and prayed to Him.

I visited the hospital again and again, and the ambulance kept driving me back to the same hospital and the same emergency room. Some of the nurses started to recognize me and smile at me. They tried to encourage me by saying that this time the doctors would definitely find the cause of my symptoms. During one such visit, they decided to do an ultrasound because they were suspicious of an abdominal problem.

The girl performing the ultrasound said, "What is this?" She pointed with the computer mouse at my left side of my back. She ran to get the doctor in the ultrasound room.

I smiled because I did not believe there could be anything seriously wrong inside of me that could be threatening my life. Even though I would cry when I was alone with my Lord, I claimed His promises in the middle of my tragedy and my uncertainties. I was fighting through my fears and negative emotions. I was smiling and telling everyone that I was fine. "I know that I am protected by the Most High God. I am His daughter. I love Jesus, and He covered me with His blood.

> If God is for us, who can be against us? (Romans 8:31 KJV)

One of my favorite preachers said, "It's okay that you are afraid sometimes. It is only proof that you are human. It would be much worse if fear had you. If you were never afraid, you would be better than Moses or any other person in the Bible."

After walking daily with my God, serving Him in our worship team and the church library, and leading a prayer group in order to get God's promises into my life, I found that instead of denying that there was an obstacle in front of me, it was better to recognize it and lift this obstacle up to God. He could help me, and I could grow more in His faith.

For my entire life, I had been pretty healthy and full of energy. The last time I was at the hospital was when I delivered my second baby more than twenty years ago. Even though family members from several generations had suffered from different types of cancer, what would family history mean if I am under covenant of my Lord? He paid the price, and by His stripes, I am healed.

Many years ago, the Holy Spirit told me through my prayers and personal time with Him, "Take my inheritance because your parents are only people who I elected in order for you to be born on this Earth. I created you, and you are my daughter. I wiped out from you all sickness as a wave of ocean cleans everything that was written on the sand. Take my inheritance."

I am healthy and blessed. I prayed and claimed that every day. I believed that nothing could harm me. There were no more curses on me. Also, as a holistic health coach, I constantly changed my meals and my lifestyle every day. I learned that most family diseases are transferred from one generation to another because of family choices and traditions like lifestyle and recipes that are given from grandmothers to daughters and granddaughters. I believed in the Word of my God, and I did my part to have the long and blessed life He promised.

No weapon formed against you will prevail. (Isaiah 54:17 NIV)

Unfortunately, this time was a different story. After the ultrasound, I was told that I had a tumor on my left adrenal gland and multiple fibroids on my uterus. They did not know what caused the nausea and assumed it was from the fibroids.

After the diagnosis, a small, slim Indian doctor from the emergency room tried to calm me down. He said that the tumor most likely was not cancerous, and it could easily be removed later. "There is nothing to worry about."

I was given more pills, and a taxi brought me back to the hotel.

In the empty hotel room, I felt like a prisoner. I was constantly tortured by my symptoms and fear. I made a choice to cleave to my God, subconsciously feeling that only He could help me overcome what I was facing at that time. In 1994, I gave my heart to the Living God in a small Ukrainian church. God gave me dreams about parts of the Bible I hadn't even read yet. I adored Him from the very first moment I found Him, and I sincerely followed Him.

God promised never to forsake me. I grew up and raised my kids with Him, and He cleaned me inside and out. He gave me His heavenly languages, visions, and songs to better understand Him and glorify His Holy Name.

I had the most happy and intimate times with God. I was learning and slowly digesting His Word every day. I was getting to know Him more each day, and I was becoming more and more thirsty for Him. Nothing could compare to or substitute for my time in His presence. There was no need to tell me about Him or about how real and alive He is. I already knew Him and trusted I was in His hands. I sincerely followed and searched for Him. I searched for His wisdom and answers to my countless questions and prayers, and each time, I found His unlimited understanding, mercy, and love.

When He filled me with His Holy Spirit, I was sharing and

encouraging people around me, but now I needed that encouragement myself.

I called people who would pray for me, including my son, Andrew, and his wife. Isadora, our adorable new family member, was originally from Hong Kong. She sincerely follows the Lord and serves Him in a small Baptist church in Calgary. My youngest baby, my daughter Alexandra, had just started to date a good guy from a Catholic church. My close girlfriend from Ukraine, Liliya, has lived in Portland with her family for many years. I tried to reach an international ministry we supported to ask for prayers, but the telephone connection was not very good. I could not connect with them.

Each morning, when I opened my eyes and my conscience turned back to my reality, my memory brought me back to where I was. The symptoms would start to prove that it was all indeed happening. Nausea and fear hit me again and again.

The hot climate and the noise from the air-conditioner, which made more noise than actual cold air, did not help me at all. I was reading the Bible alone all day, claiming His promises over myself, listening to worship music, and praying with tears on my cheeks and neck. I felt trapped in the room like a small bird in a cage. I was not able to even go outside without the presence of my husband because of the culture in the Middle East. I was afraid of being kidnapped, which had happened to other Caucasian women there. Also, I was apart from my kids, home, church, and church friends. Everything made me feel deeply isolated in the middle of my crisis. Each day, I would help my husband with his Excel spreadsheets, and if I could, I would walk or sit in the hotel's backyard to help reduce the fear and move some of my attention away from the unknown symptoms.

After a week and a half, the situation did not improve. I was having difficulty breathing and felt dizzy. I could have opened my own pharmacy because the ambulance was driving me to the hospital almost every day, and every time, I was getting more pills.

I felt the side effects of the pills—dizziness, low energy, and high blood pressure—but I did not get any benefits.

Stress made my short-term memory very bad. Stress and anxiety are bad for your body, and they are horrible for your brain too. In fact, stress and anxiety can affect your ability to maintain memories, recall memories, and even form new ones. I was not able to remember what pills I had just taken. After taking some sedatives, I was confused and disoriented.

One day, I was alone, as usual, and I started to experience heart pain and a lack of oxygen. I called the front desk and described what I was feeling. Thirty minutes later, I was being carried to the ambulance by two paramedics. The paramedics put me on a gurney and fastened me with belts because I could not walk properly.

I felt ashamed and hopeless in that big hallway in the middle of the day. The lobby was full of people who were chatting and laughing, talking on their phones, or waiting to check in. Most of the staff and management were aware that something was wrong with me. Slowly but surely, their pleasant looks turned to curiosity and then to pity. Some people were looking at me with fear, and their looks were saying, "I am so glad that it did not happen to me."

Oh, how I would have preferred to be invisible at that moment. Different thoughts were swarming in my head. I finally thought, *Who cares? What happened happened, and I can't change it now.*

The paramedics brought me back to the same hospital. After checking my file and medical history, the emergency room doctor decided to keep me at the hospital for further and more detailed diagnostics.

CHAPTER 4

With Jesus in the Arabic Hospital

In my hotel room, I created my own little world where I could have my own setting. Several times a day, I heard loud prayers to a different god all around the city.

> For thou hast been a shelter for me and a strong
> tower from the enemy. (Psalm 61:3 KJV)

From morning to evening, I was praying and worshipping my dear Jesus through www.worship.com while doing my computer work. From time to time, I would look at my watch in hopes that my husband would be back soon so I would not be alone for the rest of the day and night.

With the doctor's further diagnostics at Hamad General Hospital, I had to stay alone in these totally different surroundings. The people had different cultures, languages, and habits. Some people looked different and had different beliefs. My small world disappeared, but the Holy Spirit—my Comforter, the gift of love from my dearest Jesus who is living inside of me—was with me to prove that I was not an orphan on this earth.

> And I will ask the Father, and he will give you
> another advocate to help you and be with you
> forever—the Spirit of truth. The world cannot
> accept him, because it neither sees him nor knows
> him. But you know him, for he lives with you and
> will be in you. I will not leave you as orphans; I will
> come to you. (John 14: 16–18 NIV)

After several minutes, I was moved to the third floor where I was going to stay. The nurse put me in a wheelchair, and a special elevator brought us to a big lobby where there were many people waiting. Beside the chairs, there were small tables with tea, coffee, and pastries on a beautiful Arabic tray. After a couple of seconds, the nurse opened the door to a big room with six beds. Each bed had a curtain around it for privacy. In the middle of the room, there was a washroom. The room was divided with three beds on the right and on the left. My bed was right beside the door and the window to the narrow corridor. Opposite to my window, the doctors and nurses on duty that day sat at a table.

I closed the curtain around my bed, hoping I could make another little world to hide in. Of course, it was only an illusion. The nurses and the doctors could see me anytime through that window, and every time someone came to visit the older woman beside me, they would move the curtain to try to squeeze through to her bed. As a result, they would look at my bed. I felt like I could be seen by everyone visiting her.

I was the only Caucasian woman in the room, and there were a lot of curious looks from the Arabic visitors. They were wondering who I was. Numerous relatives were constantly supporting and comforting the older woman beside me. One day, there was a waiting line of relatives waiting outside the door with gifts for her. It was a big contrast to my situation. No one visited me since my kids were in Canada, and my husband was working. He would visit me for a short time after work.

I would lie down on my bed and pray to my dear Jesus. He is always with me—no matter what country I am in. His Spirit was with me in Ukraine ever since I gave my life to Him. His Spirit was with me in Canada, and He was with me in the Middle East—in that hospital bed. I prayed quietly with all my heart and adoration to Him. He is the One I never lost. I lost my parents many years ago, and I miss them a lot. I was the only child in my family, and the memory of my happy childhood always warms my heart. This feeling, however, was incomparable to what I have toward my dear Jesus and the Holy Spirit.

Jesus always has the ability, willingness, and faithfulness to be with me. I have trusted in Him throughout the years, and I trust Him completely.

Never will I leave you; never will I forsake you.
(Hebrews 13:5 NIV)

Doctors requested an x-ray of my chest, a CT scan of my head, a CT scan of my abdomen, and a CT scan of my whole body. I was put in a wheelchair and transferred to a different room. These procedures were not pleasant at all, and they had a hard time finding my vein to do a contrast infusion for the CT scan. They poked me with a needle several times and tried to find the vein but had no success. My veins have always been hard to find.

The CT scan machine reminded me of a coffin, but even in this machine, I was not alone. I was carrying the precious gift of everlasting love inside of me—the Holy Spirit. Feelings of fear and loneliness enveloped me, and I was not able to pray at all. I closed my eyes and repeated the name of my Savior: "Jesus." It was my SOS emergency signal to heaven's Governor. I belong to Him with all of my heart, and He was my *only* hope.

The next day brought more prayers, tears, scans, and analyses. Loud morning, afternoon, and evening prayers were filling all levels of the hospital via speakers. I would close the curtain around my bed and worship my Lord. I walked down the corridor, looked out through the big hospital window, and saw an entrance to the hospital's mosque. There was a lot of footwear outside. I thought, *I do not need to go somewhere to be with my Jesus. He is always in me, and I am in Him—and no one can separate us.*

> For I am persuaded, that neither death, nor life, nor angels, nor principalities, nor powers, nor things present, nor things to come, Nor height, nor depth, nor any other creature, shall be able to separate us from the love of God, which is in Christ Jesus our Lord. (Romans 8:38–39 KJV)

A new Arabic woman arrived in our room, but I could not see who she was because of the curtains. I just heard her voice, and she sounded very young. She was constantly begging for help from anyone beside her bed. She was terrified, vomiting, and asking for help in clear English. I realized this young girl had been raised in love and adoration, and she was experiencing a real threat to her life for the first time.

A woman with a soft, young voice tried to comfort her, and a man's voice said something in Arabic. I stayed in my bed and felt sorry for her suffering. Doctors were visiting them often and asking questions. It looked like they were trying to figure out something—without any results.

After a while, the voices disappeared. I assumed the girl was alone until she started vomiting. She turned to the woman on the opposite bed and repeatedly said, "Please help me." This poor girl wanted to find any visible support to save her life.

When I went to the washroom, I passed her bed. I looked through the open curtain and saw a slim girl who was maybe eleven or twelve years old. Her dad was sitting beside her bed, holding a book of prayers and ignoring her pleas for help. He concentrated on reading the Quran, and I could feel that he was putting all of his hope in the words of that book. He noticed that I was looking through the narrow gap, and the curtain was firmly closed when I returned from the washroom.

I only saw a few Caucasians in the entire hospital. People looked at me with curiosity and mistrust, and they kept their distance. I would talk with my husband if he was not busy after work. We both were hoping for good news: that the tumor on my left adrenal gland would not be cancerous. I was prescribed a daily intravenous infusion with water and vitamins to support me and help reduce the nausea so I could eat something.

Every day, I had to go through different scans. The doctors wanted to find out more about the horrible mass on my adrenal gland. I got back to my room after another scan and firmly closed the curtains around my bed.

As a drugless holistic practitioner and nutrition consultant, I was aware of how much damage radiation can cause. I also remembered what happened in Ukraine after the Chernobyl explosion, which was one of reasons we moved to Canada.

I was stricken by fear about the radiation I had been getting every day for several weeks in a row. When I got back to my bed after a procedure, I cried to my Jesus right when the daily Muslim prayers began at the hospital. I glorified my only Living God.

He gave me an answer right away. Oh, how marvelous He is. Soft words full of love and compassion came to my heart: "Don't worry—nothing will harm you. Remember?"

Shadrach, Meshach, and Abednego are figures from chapter 3 of the book of Daniel. The king of Babylon, Nebuchadnezzar, threw these three Hebrew men into a fiery furnace when they refused to bow down to the king's image. The three men were preserved from harm, and the king saw four men walking in the flames: "the fourth ... like the Son of God" (Daniel 3:16–28 KJV).

> When thou passest through the waters, I will be with thee; and through the rivers, they shall not overflow thee: when thou walkest through the fire, thou shalt not be burned; neither shall the flame kindle upon thee. (Isaiah 43:2–3 KJV)

In that moment, a picture from the Bible appeared in my mind. I saw the three Jews going through the oven and the flames killing the soldiers who were pushing them inside. Jesus was with them in the middle of the fire, and the fire could not touch them. They did not even smell like smoke.

The doctors kept me in the Hamad General Hospital for several days and asked if I would like to have surgery there. I decided to do further analysis and have the surgery at home in Canada.

I received a discharge summary that said:

> There is well-defined seven times 6 cm in diameter mass-like lesion with tiny calcific focus and showed patchy enhancement after intravenous contrast injection arising from the Left adrenal gland displacing. The is left kidney downward and the limiting. The tail of the pancreas upward and also compressing.

All the medical documents that prove this story is real are included in chapter 8.

Even after all the analyses and CT scans, the doctors were not sure if it was a malignant mass or not. Our hope was only in Jesus.

I was still experiencing nausea and had no appetite on top of all the stress, fear, and uncertainty. I missed my home, the place where I was happy. I missed Andrew, Isadora, Alexandra, my cats, and my blooming garden. They all seemed so far away from me. I thought, *If I get home, I will be fine and healthy.*

One day, when I was in the hotel room, Satan whispered, "You will never see your garden, and you will never hug your kids."

I cried and prayed, which was everything I could do at the time. Every day, I read, claimed the healing words from the Holy Bible from morning to evening, and listened to worship music with lifted hands.

For several weeks, I had been taking at least five or six prescribed medications. I was confused and disoriented, and I was experiencing strong dizziness, nausea, and weakness. Getting home would be a fifteen-hour flight without any support. The idea seemed crazy and impossible to realize, but we did not have another choice. I asked the Lord to give me strength and support during the long trip home. God always answers us.

> He shall call upon me, and I will answer him: I will be with him in trouble; I will deliver him. (Psalm 91:15 KJV)

CHAPTER 5

Divine Protection over My Journey Home

As soon as I went through security, I waited for a bus that would bring passengers to the airplane. A woman who was about my age began to talk to me, and I realized she was Canadian. She was flying to Calgary on the same airline. She was very kind to me, and we chatted a little about life in Doha. She offered her help and company during this trip, which encouraged me a lot.

I brought my small carry-on luggage onto the airplane and found my seat. I was exhausted as I tried to find the strength to lift my small case and put it in the overhead bin. I lifted the case with trembling hands, but it pulled me in the opposite direction. It seemed like even the case was stronger than I was. It was very embarrassing. Fortunately, the man who was sitting beside me asked if he could help me, and I gladly accepted. He was much older than me, around seventy-five, and he was slim and had black hair and dark skin. I finally dropped my powerless body into my seat with great relief.

The man who helped me with my luggage was going to be my

neighbor. We bought a business-class ticket because it was the only option to get some sleep during the long flight and refresh myself with energy; I needed to make my connecting flight in Germany. The man looked rich and sophisticated. He looked like someone who had a comfortable lifestyle. He was wearing an expensive dark blue suit and tried to make small talk with me. I was very appreciative for his help, but I had no desire to lose my last drops of energy by chatting with him. I was eager to get home and hug my kids. My son was married, but my daughter was still living with us at home. She had promised to meet me at the airport as soon as I landed in Calgary.

Regardless of my condition, I gave my neighbor permission to continue with the small talk. I soon found out that he was an Italian businessman who had several offices in Europe. He was in Doha because of his business. Soon, the nice and polite flight attendant gave us a hot towel, a menu, and nicely decorated plates with a hot meal. I forced myself to eat, even though I had no appetite, and after a couple of bites, the nausea started to bother me again. I put my spoon on my plate and tried to take a break, hoping the nausea would leave. I was really surprised when my neighbor looked like he was struggling with the same situation. I sadly thought that this seventy-five-year-old man might have digestive problems. I was a fifty-two-year-old woman who was full of energy just several weeks ago, and now I was sitting in front of my plate with the same problem.

After taking my sedatives, I fell into deep sleep. I woke up in better condition and felt like I had some energy for the next day at the airport. Although the nausea returned as soon as I opened my eyes, I nonetheless had a quick breakfast. I swallowed a handful of my pills and prepared myself for the transfer and the next flight.

The woman who was flying to Calgary was sitting in the same section. As soon as our plane landed, we carried our luggage together and tried to find the gate for our next flight in the crowded, huge Frankfurt airport. The noise, the lights, the people running in different directions with their suitcases, the constant announcements, and the shops usually entertained me, but I was overwhelmed and was not able to deal with all of it by myself. I had no interest in shopping, and I could barely understand where I needed to go for our connecting flight. I was following my new friend like a calf following her mom and trying to use my energy wisely so that I would have enough to reach my seat on the next plane.

We walked quickly with our luggage, and I did my best to hide my disoriented condition and torturous nausea. I tried to remember the information about my next flight while keeping up with our conversation. We had a couple of hours between flights, but my all energy was gone. It was summertime, and the airport was crowded with passengers who were going on vacation. We could not even find a seat. I desperately needed to drop my exhausted body somewhere, and my new friend kindly invited me to her luxury VIP service room. We found the VIP service area, and as a guest of my new friend, I was allowed to go through the entrance. The area was comfortable and quiet, and there was food. It was a nice place to rest. We had another four hours of waiting in front of us.

I am still amazed at how God was answering my prayers.

> And it shall come to pass, that before they call, I will answer; and while they are yet speaking, I will hear. (Isaiah 65:24 KJV)

Compared to a noisy public airport, it was a different world. Several polite waitresses were standing beside a fancy glass table with free refreshments and snacks. There were comfortable leather couches, small tables, and free internet. A few people were resting there quietly. There was an option of taking a shower, but I was experiencing digestive problems, a stomachache, and low energy after my pills and hours of sitting on the aircraft. I thought the shower would just make me feel weaker. I did not have enough energy to take a shower.

At that moment, I was thinking more about how I could help myself feel better and finish my trip home to Calgary. I went to the washroom, and no one else was in there. I closed the door and did an enema. As soon as I cleaned myself, I felt better. The thought that I would soon hug my daughter in the airport motivated me for the next step.

I went to our rest area, closed my eyes, and thought about how great my God is. He is always beside me, and He is always faithful.

CHAPTER 6

A Kick in the Stomach

Finally, after flying another day, I got to the Calgary airport the next evening. This was a Calgarian's favorite time—Summer Stampede—and right beside the waiting area, musicians in cowboy clothes and fancy hats were playing popular country music. People were laughing, listening to joyful music, and dancing around.

I had totally forgotten it was Stampede time. People were celebrating summertime; most of the passengers were flying to vacation or back from vacation. They were all excited and happy to hug the friends and family who were waiting for them. The spirit of celebration was around, but in front of me, there was only long fight for my life.

In the middle of noise, music, and dancing, my eyes found my baby. She was looking intensely at people and trying to find me. After a minute, our eyes finally met. I dropped my small suitcase, and we ran to each other. We tightly hugged and held hands, and tears sparkled on our eyes. All the pain and bitterness of what had happened over the past several weeks overflowed in our hearts, and we did not need to say anything. We understood each other without words. For several minutes, we could not unlock our arms to prove to ourselves that we were together again.

As soon as I got my house, I opened the door and looked at my blooming garden. It reminded me of the moment when Satan whispered to me in hotel room when I was struggling against the fear: "You will never hug your kids, and you will never see your garden."

The pain and tears came back with the memory, but I took all the strength I had at the moment and made a decision to obey God's promise instead. I stopped all my emotions. Standing on my deck, I said, "You are a liar."

> Ye are of your father the devil, and the lusts of your father ye will do. He was a murderer from the beginning, and abode not in the truth, because there is no truth in him. When he speaketh a lie, he speaketh of his own: for he is a liar, and the father of it. (John 8:44 KJV)

Huge changes had happened since I had seen my lovely kids. The diagnosis, the pain, and the phone calls and worries made us feel like we had not seen each other for several months.

I was facing a lot of praying, crying, physical and emotional pain, sleepless nights, suicidal thoughts, loneliness, and fear, but I would be dancing and worshipping my dearest Jesus even if the tears covered my neck and chest. My Savior would crucify that ugly tumor on His cross. I refused to accept the diagnosis. I was ready for my new victorious life with Jesus. He gave me miraculous healing and a second chance to live. I would enjoy each day with Him and my loved ones, and I would fulfill my destiny.

There were a lot of chapters left in my life journey. From that point on, I would be truly happy as a woman, a wife, and a mother. I would emerge victorious from pain, lies, betrayal, and cruelty. I would find my truly royal place and destiny, which my Lord prepared for me before my birth. My royal seat will wait for me until I am ready to take my place by my Savior, according to His promises for my life.

I would go victoriously through the hell and fire because of the love of the Lord. I found myself being deeply thankful for *everything* I had gone through with my precious Comforter. His gift is love—the Holy Spirit—and I will always be His daughter. I am privileged and honored to be under His blood of covenant. He is *always* faithful—even when I am not.

Life is a test. God offered me an opportunity to be faithful, strong, and honest. He offers this chance to everyone, including my family members and close friends. We choose to pass or fail and learn or refuse to learn. (You will find this story in my second book.)

I was in front of my heaviest journey, the driest desert, and the highest mountain. I was surrounded by fire and fighting for my life.

This is the beauty and difference between me and my dear Savior. His precious holy soles touched sinful ground. Mysteries will be revealed to us in the future because of His love and mercy. Jesus was perfectly aware of the agony and each drop of His precious blood from His deep wounds, but He perfectly completed the Father's will. His path saved me and healed me.

Thank You, Lord, for being merciful and for covering all my years of grief with your mystery. You made me strong and gave me time to prepare to overcome the highest mountain and fight the biggest fire in my life. Those years gave me an amazing relationship with You. Those years helped7 me get to know You better and learn from you more and more.

Thank You for loving me more than I love myself. Thank You, my sweet Holy Spirit, for Your humor and intimate time with me— without limits or appointments.

CHAPTER 7

My Family's Battle Strategy and My Miraculous Healing

I was sitting on my porch and looking at my blooming garden. The flowers I planted were blooming from early spring until the first frost in late fall. My garden always gave me strength and peace—just like it says in the Bible. It was a quiet place to read my Bible on a bench in the corner. I celebrated family events and had friends over too. On summer evenings, we had dinners and good wine by the fire pit.

God promised me that I would live a long life.

> Because he hath set his love upon me, therefore will I deliver him: I will set him on high, because he hath known my name. He shall call upon me, and I will answer him: I will be with him in trouble; I will deliver him, and honour him. With long life will I satisfy him, and shew him my salvation. (Psalm 91:14–15 KJV)

I stopped my emotions and forced myself to replace them with the words of the Living Book. I turned my back to the garden and opened the back door. I was ready to face my next battle—the battle for my life—with Jesus in Calgary, Canada.

On the day I landed, my son and daughter-in-law came to visit. I shared everything that happened with tears in my eyes. They asked what they could do? "What is the next step?"

Just before my flight to the Middle East, I had an annual checkup with my family doctor. After reviewing the results and answers to thousands of questions from the annual exam, he told me I was completely healthy. My results were actually better than most people typically have at my age. My kids read my discharge summary and the prognosis from the hospital (see chapter 13).

After giving myself a couple of days to rest and regain a bit of energy, I called my family doctor to book an appointment. He was a little older than me, and he had been born in India and raised in South Africa. He had been my doctor for six or seven years and was kind each time I saw him. Sometimes we joked and chatted about family and life.

As usual, he lifted his head, smiled, and asked me how I was doing and about my time in the Middle East. I had shared my plans for joining my husband during my last checkup. He did not expect anything to be wrong with my health. I sat down in front of his desk and said, "I am fine. Thank you."

I had been claiming what the Bible said since I felt the first symptoms in Doha:

> The Shunammite's son was passed away and woman remembered that her pregnancy was a miracle from God after being childless all her life. God gave to her son and only God is able to raise him back to life. Her faith and confidence was a much strong in God that she even did not say anything to her husband, but instead claimed "All is well."

The child sat on her lap till noon, and then he died. And she went up and laid him on the bed of the man of God and shut the door behind him and went out. Then she called to her husband and said, "Send me one of the servants and one of the donkeys, that I may quickly go to the man of God and come back again." And he said, "Why will you go to him today? It is neither new moon nor Sabbath." She said, "All is well." (2 Kings 4:20–23 KJV)

I told him everything that happened in Doha, and I gave him my chart from the Hamad hospital. I tried to keep my voice firm and calm, but my voice cracked—and a few tears came out.

He was in shock. He read over all the medical documents and said he would make an appointment with the endocrinologist. I would need to go through all the analyses and diagnostics again because—even though all of the diagnostics had been completed a week prior—Canadian doctors would not recognize it.

I went home to wait for a call from the endocrinologist.

I was in my lovely home, but even my garden was not welcoming to me anymore. My own home felt suffocating to me. Nothing was exciting to me—not even my gardening. Questions were constantly overloading my brain. I wondered what I should do now.

My kids and I were praying for a miracle every day. As soon as I landed, I called a few close friends who I had known for years. I only reached out to my friends who were strong Christians, walked daily with God, and sought His presence. They would consider my pain their own and not react emotionally. They would react spiritually, stand with me, and blindly believe in our Lord's promises more than the doctors' diagnosis.

I also called several ministries that I regularly sent financial donations, ordered materials, and listened to their preaching on TV, CD, or DVD. With these ministries, I grew spiritually day by day.

The leaders of these ministries were anointed and sensitive to the Holy Spirit, constantly experiencing the presence of the Holy Spirit. There are healing miracles in their personal lives and for thousands of people who attend their services. These ministries are Morris Cerullo, Benny Hinn, Reinhard Bonnke, and ministry of Richard Roberts (Oral Roberts's son).

After a week or so, I got a phone call from the receptionist at my family doctor's office. My first appointment with the endocrinologist would not be for a couple months.

I was shocked and asked her to try to move my first appointment sooner, but she said there was absolutely no way to do that.

Time was not on my side at that point of my life. In front of me was an entire diagnostic process—just like the one I experienced at the hospital in Hamad. I called to my son right away to figure out how we could move up the appointment.

From morning to evening, as soon as I woke up, my brain turned back to the picture of reality and my memories of what was happening with me. In that instant, the symptoms of nausea started to torture me. It was proof that everything was real. I thought, *What else I can do?* I decided to search the internet for answers.

Andrew was trying to help me get an earlier appointment, and he called our family doctor's office to talk to the receptionist. She was quite rude until he mentioned that the next step would be to contact a college patient advocate and make a complaint. The next day, she called and gave me an appointment with the endocrinologist for the next week.

Andrew and I went to the South Health Campus Hospital. Before seeing the doctor, we went to the nurse. She opened a file for me and added all the information about the pills I was taking from the Hamad Hospital. There were five or six prescription drugs that should have helped with my condition and suppressed the nausea, but nothing seemed to work. I was weak, drowsy, and constantly nauseous. It reminded me of my pregnancies.

After seeing the nurse, I stared at the door and prayed in my heart for a miracle. Before walking inside the hospital, my son and I prayed in the car. We hoped that something was wrong with Hamad's diagnostics and that it would be proven here in Canada that it was definitely not cancer. After some treatments, I would be fine.

Finally, the door opened, and a young woman with blonde hair smiled and invited us to come in. After introducing herself, she carefully checked my nails, hands, and tongue and asked me several questions. She already reviewed the discharge summary from the Hamad General Hospital, and she was quite optimistic. At the end of the appointment, she said, "We do scientific research on adrenal gland issues, and I can swear on my house that it is not a cancerous tumor."

We took the medical requisitions, analysis, and scans and left the hospital.

My son said, "See? Nothing to worry about. After the diagnostics, the doctor said there are two options: treatment or surgery. I think they will give you some treatments, and the tumor will dissolve."

After a week or so, I got a phone call from the hospital. The soft voice of a nurse, a well-trained professional who dealt with high-stress patients told me the date and time of my appointment for a PET-CT scan and the preparation instructions. She repeated the information several times. A PET scan is a test that uses a small amount of radioactive material to detect different diseases in the body, such as cancer, while a CT scan requires x-ray equipment and a contrasting material for detailed images of the body.

I was worried that I would need to go through a CT scan and have more radiation. In the Hamad hospital, I had x-rays and CT scans of my head, abdomen, and body. Being originally from Ukraine and going through Chernobyl, I was perfectly aware of what radiation could do for human health and the environment. After Chernobyl, the population in Ukraine experienced a rapid increase in the number of cancer patients, mostly kids. Hospitals were overloaded, and statistics proved that more people were dying than were born. Radioactive decay could continue for thousands of years, and people who could move away did. That was the main reason my family decided to immigrate to Canada. The worry settled into my head, but I substituted it with a place from the Bible that the Holy Spirit pointed out to me in the hospital in the Middle East.

> "No weapon that is formed against thee shall prosper; and every tongue that shall rise against thee in judgment thou shalt condemn. This is the heritage of the servants of the Lord, and their righteousness is of Me," saith the Lord. (Isaiah 54:17 KJV)

I went through a CT scan with a contrast injection. God gave me very tiny veins, so it usually took the nurses couple of tries to get one. As I entered the CT scan machine, I closed my eyes and repeated my Savior's name: "Jesus. Jesus."

After several days, we went back to the endocrinologist's office at the hospital. We had gone through the nurse's room, and our appointment should have started quite a while ago, but the doctor's door was still closed. Based on the last conversation with her, my son was calm. I was silently praying for a good result. We were sitting quietly, but different thoughts were in my mind. We claimed the promises of healing in our hearts and kept our lips shut. Another ten or fifteen minutes passed, but the door remained closed. I could clearly hear the doctor talking on the phone with someone. Finally, we were inside.

A young endocrinologist was welcoming, but I recognized the tension on her face. She started with the good news, telling us that she already talked with one of the leading surgeons from the Foothills Hospital. She specialized in adrenal glands and had already transferred all of my medical results. Even though patients usually waited months for an appointment with her, she was ready to see me next week. We were glad to hear it. We didn't understand right away why such a busy surgeon—who dedicated her time to saving patients' lives and to science—was going to see me so quickly.

After the good news, the doctor said that she received the result from all of my analyses. "Unfortunately, it is a cancerous tumor, eight centimeters in diameter, on your left adrenal gland. The adrenal gland is only one centimeter."

My son and I were in shock.

She said, "I am very sorry, but I don't have anything else to tell you."

After several seconds, she told me that I needed to go through more scans for them to gain more information about the tumor and verify that the organs around the left adrenal gland were clean— without any metastases. She said that it looked like it was the only tumor, but I would need to go through more scans and analyses to check my bones as well. She was very careful with her words to make sure she wasn't saying anything definite without any proof yet.

Even though we stayed silent and composed, the news was like a kick in the stomach. I felt like I had been hit, and my heart rate felt like I was running a marathon. I started to sweat, and everyone knows how strong stress sweat is. I felt embarrassed, and the tears came out.

After several minutes of silence, I started to question the possibility of it all being a mistake. I asked her about the bet she made on her house that it was most likely not cancerous.

She said that the adrenal protocol sometimes could not be diagnosed.

I asked about the annual checkup I had before leaving, and the answer was that cancer sometimes is not possible to see through blood analysis.

My son asked her something, and she answered something. I tried to understand but I could not. I was frozen and felt like a statue, which happened to me several times when my dear parents passed away. You cannot get used to that feeling. Finally, my brain seemed to accept the information, and I understood the meaning of the words around me.

Andrew was asking about the next appointment and any information about my adrenal gland that could help us.

We sat with the doctor for quite a while, and the nurse came in to let the doctor know the next patient was waiting. We left the room without saying anything else, took to the elevator, and got inside the car.

Andrew closed the door, and we sat in silence and processed everything.

I asked, "What are we going to do now?"

At the time, Andrew was thirty-one years old. He had just gotten married to a beautiful Christian girl and celebrated their one-year anniversary. He and his wife lived in a new home that was close to their work. They dedicated their time to helping a local Baptist church in Calgary. We were excited to have more family members and grandchildren. My daughter, Alexandra, named after my dad, was twenty-three, and I was dreaming about her wedding one day. She was dating a guy from good family, and we had already met them.

My husband and I were happy. Just several months ago, he had gotten down on his knee and proposed to me again—even though we'd been married for more than thirty years. I was the happiest woman in the world. We were thinking about retirement, grandkids, and a possible relocation to British Columbia in the future. Life was full of plans and joyful expectations for tomorrow, but this news turned everything upside down unexpectedly. My husband was still finishing the project in the Middle East, but my son and daughter were there to support me. I also spent time with the sweet Holy Spirit every day.

Driving home was quiet. I was not really ready to say my thoughts out loud because I believed that "death and life are in the power of the tongue" (Proverbs 18:21 KJV).

Before we got home, my husband called to my son to ask about the result of the CT scan and the doctor's appointment. He had just landed in Calgary and was trying to contact us from the airport. We were almost home—just one more block left. After thirty-five minutes of driving from the hospital to our home, we were still in shock. My son could not simply repeat what we had just learned about my condition while he was driving. We decided to wait until my husband got home from the airport.

We believed our endocrinologist's assurances that the tumor was most likely not cancerous. My kids, my friends, and I were all praying and claiming the promises of life over me daily.

Since I landed in Calgary, I did not watch TV or entertain myself with shopping or parties. All my time was spent with Jesus, His Word, and prayers and worship. My family and I were in a position of war with Satan. He had attacked me, and I was on the battlefield.

I used sticky notes to write the promises of health, longevity, and everything else the Holy Spirit pointed out to me when I was reading the Bible. I searched my heart and asked the Holy Spirit to show me any obstacles to my healing. I asked for forgiveness, and I forgave everyone who put pain in my heart. I did not know what else I could do, and I did not have an answer for why my expectations had not been fulfilled.

I deeply believe that God—who I have loved and adored since I was saved in 1994, the year when my mom passed away from colon cancer at fifty-nine years old—is alive. In 1994, before I opened the Bible and started to read the Book of Life, God gave me a dream that my family would move to a better house. In the new house, I was able to see how my first home collapsed when heavy rains covered it and the mud under the concrete moved. When I was watching that destruction, I thought, *How is it possible that I was living in that house and did not see it. The house looked so firm and stable.*

The second pastor from my church in Ukraine said, "Wow. This is from the Bible." He showed me a place in the Bible that described the same scenario. I started to read the Bible and question everything. Every time I was in church or a cell group, I found the pastor or his assistant and asked them endless questions.

He opened his Bible and read to me:

> Everyone then who hears these words of mine and does them will be like a wise man who built his house on the rock. And the rain fell, and the floods came, and the winds blew and beat on that house, but it did not fall, because it had been founded on the rock. And everyone who hears these words of mine and does not do them will be like a foolish man who built his house on the sand. And the rain fell, and the floods came, and the winds blew and beat against that house, and it fell, and great was the fall of it. (Matthew 7:24–27 ESV)

From the moment I accepted Jesus in my heart, I was saved. I fell in love with Him badly and sincerely. After being baptized, I got spiritual gifts—heaven languages—which Jesus promised us:

> All of them were filled with the Holy Spirit and began to speak in other tongues as the Spirit enabled them. (Acts 2:4 NIV)

> When Paul placed his hands on them, the Holy Spirit came on them, and they spoke in tongues and prophesied. (Acts 19:6 NIV)

I began to learn about God the Father, His Son, and the Holy Spirit through His Word and by spending time with Him. Being born in the former USSR, I was raised to believe that Lenin was the most kind and honest person in the world. He defended poor people, loved kids, and dedicated his life to other people. I found out that Lenin is not the best—God is. He is alive, and He is Spirit. He is the only One who is perfect. He is the real God—not Lenin.

Besides the Orthodox churches, icons, and traditional celebrations for Easter and Christmas, there actually exists a daily connection with God through His Word and Spirit. I started to seek His face daily. My soul was thirsty for Him for such a long time. I started to pray in tongues, and God began to give me visions, dreams, prophecies, and songs. He started to clean me inside and out. I was born again and had a new life. I was in love with Him, and I soon became involved in worship, prayer service, church library, and home cell groups. I was not perfect, but I sincerely followed my Lord with a heart full of love and adoration of Him.

So many questions were filling my brain. I was asking the Holy Spirit questions all day and all night. *What is wrong now? Why won't God answer our family's prayers right away? Why didn't we get the miracle we were expecting?*

As time passed, I had more questions than answers. I would get the answers—not in my timing but in His. It was a time of learning and knowing Him more than before. It was time for obedience, patience, and growing in Him.

CHAPTER 8

Following God's Promises, the Spiritual War Begins

The three of us were sitting at home after the appointment with the endocrinologist. My son, my husband, and I got the terrible news about the cancerous tumor on my left adrenal gland—despite the doctor's assurances in Doha and the endocrinologist's visual diagnosis in Canada. My daughter was in university and was not aware of the recent bitter news in our family.

All of our family members were Christians. We believe in God's miracles and His promises. After landing to Calgary, we were praying and claiming the good news regarding the results of the MRI. Our youngest family member, my daughter, was confident that the MRI would prove to be the answer for God's healing miracle for me.

My baby was ten years old when she had a vision from God before we immigrated to Canada. More than ten years ago, it was a big decision to move to new country without relatives or money and start a new life from nothing at forty years old with two kids. After seeking answers and guidance from the Lord regarding immigration, God chose her to give the answer through a dream that would encourage us to immigrate. A huge ocean wave was coming from the deep water and was ready to swallow us. The wave looked like a tsunami. Our family was staying in the water, up to our ankles, and we joined hands and started to pray.

Now she was a university student, but she saved her child's belief and trust in God for her mom's healing. She was the one who was crying and scared for me when I was in Doha and asking for her prayers for my weird symptoms. After drying her tears, said bravely to her Catholic boyfriend, "We believe in God's healing—so let's pray." Now my baby was the only one who was at university. She sincerely believed that God had already answered our prayers—and the MRI had already proved it.

As soon as the taxi brought my husband home from the airport, my son repeated to him everything the doctor had said. A lot of events and pain had happened in the past couple weeks, and it seemed like months had gone by.

I was exhausted and could not even actively participate in the conversation. I was sitting quietly on the sofa and trying to figure out what was next. In the middle of the talk, my daughter found a moment to call after her class. The news was so dramatic for the whole family that my son did not tell her the results of the MRI until she was back at home.

When all of us were finally home, we were perfectly aware of the meaning of what the doctor had said. Different thoughts swarmed in my head and in all of our heads. We tried to digest everything and figure out what we needed to do next.

Our house was full of Christian books, CDs, and DVDs about the Living God who performs miracles in people's lives and resurrects the dead to glorify His Holy Name.

Since I lost my mom when she was fifty-nine years old to colon cancer—and since the moment I gave my life to Jesus—the Holy Spirit has led me to learn more and more about the supernatural power of God and His will to heal His people. I remember the moment when my mom was in the hospital many years ago. The doctor said that they could not help her. It was too late.

I was in despaired. I sat beside her bed while she was sleeping under the morphine and said, "Who can help us?"

I saw a shadow in the twilight on the door of her private room. Right away, I said, "Can you help us?"

There was no answer. I contacted several famous doctors to get a second opinion and help save my mom's life, but no one could do it. In the same year that my mom passed away, I gave my life to dearest Jesus. I was thrilled that I had found the answer to my question about who could do supernatural healing.

Every time I found out anything about miracle healing or resurrection by the Holy Spirit, it held a special meaning for me. I was aware who could help in hopeless situations and who had unlimited power. I am His loyal daughter through the blood of Jesus, and all His promises for healing from Bible are mine.

> And thou shalt speak unto the children of Israel, saying, if a man die, and have no son, then ye shall cause his inheritance to pass unto his daughter. (Numbers 27:8 KJV)

> The king's daughter is all glorious within: her clothing is of wrought gold. With gladness and rejoicing shall they be brought: They shall enter into the king's palace. (Psalm 45:13, 15 KJV)

Daughter. This special word has always been full of meaning for me. I was the only daughter in my family, and my childhood was full of memories of love and joyful moments. My dad was a talented doctor and a kind person, and he always had time to be with me— no matter how busy he was. When I was a child, I could pass the waiting line in the clinic and open the door to his office because he was my dad. I was recognized by people as a doctor's daughter, and I was so proud of him.

Many people called our home to ask for his help and to book appointments with him, but I did not need any appointment because he was my daddy. Daddy loved me deeply—always and unconditionally. He was my friend and the most trustworthy person. He always protected me and was ready to understand and support me.

When I was a teen, I once asked if he would be willing to give his life to save his child.

Without even a second of hesitation, he said, "Yes."

When I had appendix surgery at seventeen years old, he wrote a poem where he expressed his love and his deep desire to take my place on the surgeon's table. Both of my dear parents have passed away now.

I now have a heavenly Father who is holy. He has no limits, and His love never ends. The Father is always alive and is always with me. It always makes me feel privileged to be named His daughter.

My previous life—growing in God, serving Him, raising our kids in our Ukrainian church, and teaching them to see that Jesus is the Lord of our life at home every day—was all in preparation for this battle. The battle tested us, taught us, and made each of us stronger and more faithful.

Get the victory or fail it. This was the choice for each of our family members. It was not just for me because the pressure and shock turned our worlds upside down, and it was not easy to overcome it and live with it for days and months. Even though we were all together as a family, each of us went through our own personal tests—equipped by the Lord, depending on our own personal time with the Lord, and walking with Him in faith and honesty.

> Therefore put on the full armor of God, so that
> when the day of evil comes, you may be able to stand
> your ground, and after you have done everything,
> to stand. (Ephesians 6:13 NIV)

During a family meeting, we came up with strategy for victory. No matter what the news is from the doctors, we will trust God for a miracle healing. We were keeping in mind my daughter's vision that God gave her many years ago. We did exactly the same thing: held hands, stood in a circle, prayed, lifted up to our heavenly Father through the name of Jesus, and prayed for a miracle healing.

CHAPTER 9

God's Miracle in Action

Thus saith the Lord unto you, Be not afraid
nor dismayed by reason of this great multitude;
for the battle is not yours, but God's.
—2 Chronicles 20:15 (KJV)

In that moment, we announced a spiritual war in our family and home. My daughter put aside dating to be with me daily, praying and supporting me to be strong in this battle.

I proclaimed the promises of healing. If human nature brought tears to my eyes, I tried to hide them from her. It was the beginning of the summer—and she had summer holidays at school—she spent most of her time with me. She was always around me, and it was difficult to hide my tears from her.

The battle began every morning daily, and my daughter always kept an eye on me. She was always checking on what I was doing and how I was behaving.

One morning, I was silently fighting with my thoughts regarding the future. *Will I be at my daughter's wedding one day?* I went into the kitchen, and my daughter looked at me and understood me without words. She said, "Do you need a hug, Mom?" I told her that I wanted to be at her wedding.

She held me tightly and said: "Mom, I believe that you will be there."

My baby dried my tears and gave me hugs whenever and as much as I needed them. We sometimes stood in the middle of the kitchen and hugged each other and cried. We could not change anything in the present, but we could trust God and wait for His answer—in His time and not ours.

We listened to preaching three or four times per day. We watched DVDs, shouted to God, and proclaimed His promises for my healing. As long as I am alive, I will remember everything about how my family and friends supported me while I faced my daily battle through the valley of grief and pain.

After some additional scans and blood tests, I had my first appointment with the general surgeon. She was a scientist, a professor, and one of the most famous surgeons in North America. She had a waiting list of up to six months, but I got an appointment only after one week of waiting. She was a nice-looking woman, approximately my age, in good shape, and a little smaller than me. She was very confident, extremely organized, and had a strong will, which my previous endocrinologist had mentioned. She was welcoming—but not very social. Her questions were clear, short, and straight to the point.

I knew right away that this woman knew how to work efficiently and valued her time. She asked about my symptoms and how everything began, and she listened very closely, trying not to miss any details. She did a physical examination and explained the results of the new scans and the blood tests. She said they did not have much information about adrenal cancer, but she specialized in the endocrinology system. According to the scan results, it is only one tumor, but she wanted to do another scan to check my bones and hormones. Because the tumor was big—eight centimeters on a tiny one-centimeter adrenal gland—surgery would be more efficient than treatment. There were many organs nearby, and it was not wise to waste time on a treatment that might not be effective.

At the hospital—where I spent most of my time—I saw people in different stages of sickness and health. After a while, I was able to recognize who the cancer patients were and who the extremely sick people were. Seeing this brought me to a point where I would be fighting against what I saw versus what I believed.

> For we walk by faith, not by sight. (2 Corinthians 5:7 KJV)

I proclaimed the words of life and trusted God in His promises every day. My family and close friends waited for my doctor's appointment. There was no chatting or laughing in our home. It was a time of spiritual war in my life. The only effective weapon was the Holy Bible, His Word, which I had mostly memorized by that point.

It had been more than fifteen years since the Holy Spirit told me to learn and memorize his Living Word from the Bible. He compared His word to bullets when cowboys fight with the enemy. I don't know why the Holy Spirit chose to remind me of a cowboy fight, but I understood the meaning right away. He reminded me of a picture I saw for American movies in the USSR. The victorious one could operate his gun masterly and kill his enemies in all directions—no matter how many of them were against him. Only when I operate my word like a master will I have more victory in my life. I started to write my dairy, read slowly, and write the Word of God that the Holy Spirit highlighted for me. At the moment when I was facing this sickness, I copied many books and pages from the Bible. My notes were my spiritual bread from a different moment of my life.

Even then, I was not completely strong and fearless. All my strength was only in Him, and I was very happy to finally go home. My son was always with me at all my appointments. He made sure I didn't miss any important information and would drive back to work after my appointments.

The news that it was a cancerous tumor affected everyone in the family. Right away, all plans and projects became a low priority. It was like an instant reflex to fight in an extreme situation. Besides praying and going through the doctor's visits, my son and I tried to find more information about the disease. I googled my case to better understand what was going on with me. I found a lot of scary and negative information and testimonies from people who were diagnosed with the same health problem as I was. I found a blog and communication from people who had been told they would only live several months or a year. Another young woman shared that two years after a tumor and her left adrenal gland were removed, her right adrenal gland got a tumor again—and the doctors didn't know what to do with her.

I studied anatomy and found out how important adrenal glands are for hormones. They are necessary for the function of many organs, including the heart. People who had been diagnosed with adrenal carcinoma were desperate for any information from anybody's experience because of how rare the disease was. Many of them were almost screaming at the internet, helplessly asking for any helpful information.

After reading these stories, horror hugged me in a cold death embrace. I called my son to share what I had found.

He listened me quietly and then said, "I know. I read all of them and more. I was searching on the computer until two o'clock last night."

For several nights—with a full-time job and a recent marriage—he had spent hours trying to find any information that could help to his mom. His eyes were constantly red when he visited me after work. "Mom, let's stop searching. I know these stories, but that is not your story. These stories make your faith weak, and I will stop searching as well. If you need any information to be prepared for one of your next scans, I will do it for you."

We agreed to substitute stories from the internet with miracle stories from Jesus that the Bible described.

My first visit to my surgeon was in the spring, and I was scheduled for surgery at the end of October. My doctor was very busy, and in front of me was a long, endless time of waiting for the moment when this disgusting tumor would be removed from my body. I felt like I was carrying a bomb inside me.

My daily schedule consisted of getting up in the morning, and as soon as I woke up, I was attacked by reality. Tears dropped from my eyes, and I would loudly say the memorized words of life from the Bible. I always kept my Bible beside my bed, and I still do it now. My Bible was full of notes, and I highlighted words until I was full of my spiritual breakfast.

After reading, I started to pray with all my heart with love and adoration to my Lord. I was sitting or kneeling and waiting for a word from Him. When I was ready to get up, the gentle Holy Spirit sometimes gave me a feeling that something was coming: "Wait." I would soon get a vision, some words, or just a warm, tender breath of love and compassion. I was then ready to begin my day despite the constant nausea of my present condition.

One morning, as I was kneeling in my bedroom, I lifted my prayer to the Lord in tears. I was waiting for the Lord in silence and heard the words: "Open your laptop and search the schedule for miracle service from Benny Hinn ministry."

My laptop was right beside me. I did it right away and found that Pastor Benny Hinn would be in Montreal the following weekend for one of his healing miracle crusades. Even though I believed in miracles and had called ministries to ask for a healing miracle, this thought had never crossed my mind. I ran to my husband and—inspired by the Word of God—convinced him that God had a plan for my healing. My husband, my daughter, and I took a flight to Montreal.

The big convention center was full of people who had been waiting in line for hours in hopes of getting a good seat that was close to the stage. Finally, we were there, and I was worshipping God with my family. I was expecting healing from the Holy Spirit at any moment. Many people were around me, and most of them were there because they were desperate for a miracle. Some of them were in wheelchairs, and some were in beds with oxygen masks. I thought, *Oh, Lord, will I even have a chance to ask for a personal prayer?*

During the first break, I waited in a line for a personal prayer from a woman who was pretty and maybe ten years older than me. She was dressed very well, and she was sitting, talking, and praying for sick people. It was very easy to miss her place in the line because everyone was just sitting in the row. I thought people were simply sitting down and not waiting in line.

A woman in the washroom told me that somebody from the Benny Hinn team was praying for healing in one of the rooms. God again gave me a direction to get what he had already done on the cross for me. Despite this, I could not get a personal prayer since the break was over. After the second part of the service, no one was praying for people. I was discouraged, but I was still full of the presence and adoration for the Lord.

I found a hotel that was close to the airport. At the end of the day, we talked about the service and shared our thoughts about how we could get a personal prayer in the large crowd.

At breakfast the next morning, my daughter pointed out the woman from the Benny Hinn team. She was having breakfast with younger blonde woman. We walked up to their table, introduced ourselves, and expressed our joy about being there.

As we were talking, the blonde woman asked me if I spoke Russian, and we found out that she was from Russia. After I explained the reason why we were there, the woman who was praying recognized me from the waiting line. She asked how long it would be until I could receive a healing prayer. This beautiful woman with big blue eyes and sophisticated dress suddenly took my hands and started to kiss them right there in the restaurant. Her voice was humbled, and the tears in her eyes showed me that she had spent quality time with the Holy Spirit. Her heart was soft and full of compassion. I was completely aware of where it came from and who was transforming her and anointing her. It was the magic touch of the Holy Spirit—the gift of love from our Lord. I knew that because it happened to me every time I was with the Holy Spirit in Ukraine or in Canada.

When I tried to ask about the possibility of having a prayer now, a woman in the waiting line said, "We are all here to get a prayer."

In that moment, for the first time, I said, "I have cancer." Even after the doctors told me that the tests showed it was a cancerous tumor, I never said it out loud. I had never accepted the diagnosis in my mind. I always thought about these words from the Bible: "Life and death depend on your tongue."

Cancer. This short word made many people in the church look at me with fear, and it was a convincing answer to the woman in the line. However, once the short break between services was over, I did not have time to ask for a prayer.

Shortly after I explained why I was there, the prayer leader told me that before he could give me access to a personal prayer from Benny Hinn on the stage, he would need to see that the Holy Spirit had touched me. He told me to come to him the next day during a break. He would be praying for a healing, and he would pray for me.

The next day, the presence of God was very strong. During the worship time, I felt electricity in my fingers. I lifted my heart to my God, worshipping him and glorifying Him with tears in my eyes.

After the first part of the service, I found a woman who was leading healing prayers, but a waiting line of people surrounded her again.

She recognized me right away and told me to watch how God would make a miracle. In front of her, there was a senior Asian woman who was almost deaf. Her relatives were translating for her and shouting each word into her ear.

After a short prayer, my new friend and sister in Christ from Benny Hinn's team asked her to check the results of the healing. She repeated a short prayer, and the next test result showed that the Asian woman could even hear whispers.

She turned to me and said, "Do you believe?"

I said, "Yes."

She said, "Check yourself, and if you feel the Holy Spirit touching you—and you feel some improvements—tell me."

I said a short prayer, but I did not feel anything right away. After the service, I didn't feel anything except the joy of being in the presence of the Holy Spirit. There was one day left, and I asked the security team how I could have a personal prayer with Benn Hinn.

They told me that he was very busy and had already left the room where the service was.

I explained that I had flown from Calgary because I had a cancerous tumor, but I got the same answer: "He is not available now." I was in shock. There were so many sick people with their own stories and their own pain. Some of them were with their parents, some were with their kids, and some were in wheelchairs. A few people were in hospital beds with life-support systems. Getting a personal prayer from Benny seemed impossible. I felt like I was a small coin in a big ocean. I thought that God had given me direction and faith. He convinced me and my family to fly to Montreal. We withdrew money for this trip, but where was the answer? There should have been an answer; God promised to heal me.

I shared my thoughts with my daughter, and she told me that the woman had prayed for me. "If this is God's will, the healing will come."

If was not in my vocabulary at that moment. It was a moment for fighting for my own life, and my survival instinct was telling me to cleave to God and to God's words. *If* could be allowed in a situation where I had something on my heart that I did not reveal to God, but I searched myself and did not find anything that would have been an obstacle to my healing. I was expecting my miracle without any *if.*

> For all the promises of God in him are yea, and
> in him Amen, unto the glory of God by us. (2
> Corinthians 1:20 KJV)

When I was driving in Calgary and saw construction of a new train station, bridge, or highway, I thought, *Am I going to see the end of this construction?* I stopped those thoughts in my mind and repeated the healing promises again and again. I used the same spiritual exercises to change my thoughts to Bible promises.

The next day was our last day in Montreal. I woke up and was listening to worship inside of me. The songs were glorifying Jesus even at night. The same worship that we had during the day continued when I was sleeping. I asked my daughter, and she said that she had the same feeling.

> Do you not know that your bodies are temples of the Holy Spirit, who is in you, whom you have received from God? You are not your own. (1 Corinthians 6:19 KJV)

When the worship began, I found that I had no pressure on the left side on my back where the tumor was. I shared this joyful news with my new friends from the Benny Hinn service, and they put me in the waiting line on the stage. I went to the stage with a man who had been diagnosed with the last stage of cancer several years ago. After many prayers, he still was in good energy and health—even though the doctors had given him only months to live.

Pastor Benny turned to me and asked what was wrong with me. I said, "Adrenal cancer."

He asked where, and I pointed to the left side of my back. I said, "It is eight centimeters long."

He rebuked the tumor in the name of Jesus, and I felt a kick from the strength and power of the Holy Spirit. I fell down on the stage and stayed there for several seconds.

Benny said, "You need one more prayer."

Two men lifted me, and after a short prayer, I was almost unconscious again. I felt the healing power the God who I had followed since my mom passed away from colon cancer in 1994.

Many people were praying for me, and I was praying for many people as well. I had flown and driven to many Christian conferences in different cities and countries, but I had never experienced such a presence and such power of the Holy Spirit.

The next morning, I went to have a complimentary breakfast in the hotel. I was usually embarrassed about fighting to swallow each bite as other people enjoyed their meals. At breakfast, I had several bites. I was still cautious since I had suffered from strong nausea for several months. I did not even realize that I was eating without nausea. I was eating carefully and slowly.

My dearest daughter was watching me and suddenly said, "Mom, you are eating."

I was eating my breakfast normally, and the nausea has never bothered me since that time. The doctors had no idea where the nausea came from or why it disappeared. Only my heavenly Doctor—dear Jesus—was aware, and He made it work on the cross.

We flew home, and the spirit inside of me was glorifying Lord with songs from the Benny Hinn worship service. The nausea was gone, and I wondered if the next scan would show no tumor and clear organs. *How is my Lord going to answer? It is always His way—and not mine.*

When we got home, the surgery was still in front of me. It was a long time to wait. I had to wait for the entire summer and the beginning of fall. My surgery was scheduled for the end of October. It was the most difficult time of my life. My flesh was fighting with my spirit inside of me every day, and my reflection in the mirror showed the image of a sick woman. The words of healing promised a substitute for what I saw.

There was a lot of pressure on my daughter and my husband because of what I was going through, and we all had a choice to grow in Him or deny Him and live by our ways and beliefs. It is always a personal choice. The words of my doctor tortured me: "There are many vitally important organs around the tumor."

I depended on the words of the Bible as sick people depend on life-support systems—twenty-four hours per day—by reading, listening, thinking about, and claiming His Word. I was exhausted from months of waiting. I went to the emergency room and asked if they could move my surgery to an earlier date. The doctor did an

MRI and told me that the tumor had enlarged—but not by much. The nausea had disappeared, but the tumor had not.

I was watching Kathryn Kuhlman videos, and she would say that she still did not understand the miracle of healing of different people in different ways. Sometimes it is not because of faith, but it is only God's business. He is the healer. One day, when I stand before Him, I will ask why not all people are healed.

It was the end of October, and it was my surgery day. My whole family was in the hospital at five o'clock in the morning to support me and pray.

The surgeon told us that it would be a five- or six-hour surgery, hopefully without complications. She said, "Even though we did a lot of tests and analyses, we are still not sure what is going on inside. I need to check all the organs to be sure the cancer did not spread around. The tumor is big, and the organs are very close."

Several days before, I had signed the release forms. I was aware of the possible complications—and even the chance of death.

After doing the checkups with the rest of the hospital staff, I went to the presurgery room to take off my clothes.

The nurse told me I needed to walk to the surgery room, and the team of doctors would deal with me. I would get an IV and fall asleep. I said goodbye to my family and kissed my kids, my daughter-in-law, and my husband. I left small studs in my ears, but the nurse said it would be better to give them to my family. I had nothing from this world. I was totally naked—the same as the day I was born—and I was ready to be born again after God performed His miracle on the table.

When I opened the door, I saw a big, bright room with many people, medical equipment, and a surgical bed. I had been told that my cancer still needed to be studied a lot since only one hundred cases existed in the world, including my case. I thought, *Maybe that is why there are so many people in the room.* I did not pay much attention to the people, but I noticed that my surgeon was not there. I focused on the surgical bed and the IV stands, and the nurses started to talk to me. A nurse explained the anesthesia process and said that my surgeon was preparing for the surgery and was coming. Two nurses recognized the fear in my eyes.

I was so scared. I whispered, "I do not even have grandkids yet. Please do your best."

My surgeon came in, saw my tears, and asked what happened. This strong, confident woman showed her deep compassion in her heart and said softly, "No worries. I will do everything I can."

It took all of my strength to lie down on that surgical bed. My body would be opened, and they would search for the answers. I had nothing on besides my surgical gown and fell asleep, giving my angels a place to guard me.

My friends and family were praying for a miracle.

I woke up in the intensive care unit. I was drowsy, and there were IVs and other machines around me. I was breathing through an oxygen mask. I really don't remember much except the ceiling, the walls, and the noise on my way to my first room in the hospital after the surgery.

After I was moved to a new bed, a pretty nurse gave me encouraging words and explained where I was. She was in her twenties, tall, and had dark brown hair. Her kind smile reflected a willingness to help. She explained to me that I would stay in an intensive care unit to get the best support and care. My surgeon would visit me soon. Everything was all right with me.

There were four more beds in the room, and another woman was beside me. Her husband was sitting and talking with her. The nurse was constantly coming in and talking to the people in the room. Each bed had a curtain around it, but it did not help with the noise. I put my second pillow on top of my head and fell asleep.

Someone took my pillow, and I opened my eyes.

My surgeon and a couple of other doctors were standing beside my bed. She was smiling and looked very happy. She said, "You are fine. I searched all the organs around your left adrenal gland. They are all clear, no spreads. I removed the eight-centimeter tumor and your left adrenal gland. We will send the cancerous tumor for a biopsy. We do not know what it is yet, but it doesn't belong to you anymore. I need to fly to New York for an International Conference, but my assistant will keep an eye on you."

I was so happy to hear that God had given me a second chance to live and see my family, but I was not able to express my feelings much. Before I fell asleep again, I said, "Thank you. Thank you. Thank you."

My family came for a short visit. My kids, my daughter-in-law, and my husband kept smiling at me and telling me that I was fine. Only the eyes of my baby, my youngest daughter were different. You don't need words to know the feelings of your kids. You gave birth to them, and you see them with your heart.

Being under so much medication, I could not talk too long with them before I fell asleep. Later, my daughter said that it was good that I did not see myself. It was a big change. I hadn't even looked in a mirror since the surgery. I felt sorry that I had scared my daughter since she is the youngest in the family. My son and daughter-in-law were much more mature and stronger.

Right after visiting my family, the nurse came in and started to explain the IVs I had. She told me that I was breathing oxygen via a support system. An IV with morphine was connected to my back, close to my spine. The other IV had my water and food for the next several days. They also had access to an artery in my neck for an emergency IV that could save my life. I was connected to a catheter. Being under the morphine and completely oblivious to my current condition, I was joyfully telling the nurse my plans for the next several days: get my hair done and get a pedicure and manicure. I was completely ignoring what she had just told me, but she just smiled.

The nurse helped me stand and take slow steps toward the washroom for the first time after the surgery. I was in a happy mood and joked about attending the spa soon. Later, I understood that it was just the morphine talking. It reminded me of my mom before she passed away since she had morphine injections for the pain.

The nurse moved me to the washroom to wash my hands, and she left me alone for some privacy. After several steps, I realized how weak I was. I looked in the mirror and noticed how skinny I was too. *Who is that?* The big blue robe made me look even skinnier. I looked at the reflection. I left my walker and grabbed the sink for support. The nurse had told me to open my robe and clean myself with a wet cloth. I slowly opened the robe and saw metal surgical clenches like a large zipper from between my breasts down to my pubic bone. There was a huge incision in the middle of my body. I had no clue that I had been opened up from top to bottom and how big the scar was going to be. My holistic doctor had thought I might have a small incision from the back. My surgeon had said that she would need to make an incision on my belly, cutting through all the muscles. I was expecting a small scar at the bottom, similar to the one I had from my appendix surgery when I was a teenager. What I saw in the mirror was a reflection of how my surgeon had been so meticulous and diligent about checking all of my organs to save my life. What I saw in mirror proved what a miracle my dear Jesus had performed in my life.

I was staring at my reflection and was not able to move my eyes from the mirror. I got a numb feeling and worried that I might pass out. I did not want to fall on the floor after surgery with fresh stitches along my whole body. I called my nurse and asked her to bring me back to my bed.

I had never passed out or been under anesthesia. Even during the appendix surgery when I was seventeen years old, I was awake and only had painkiller injections.

After calling for the nurse four or five times, she finally came in. I told her that I couldn't stand and that I was close to unconsciousness. I didn't want to see my reflection, and I asked her to bring me back to bed. The nurse calmed me down and said that we would try again after I rested.

I slowly moved back to my bed, feeling embarrassed since everyone in the room had heard my panic attack in the washroom. I kept saying that I was sorry and that I was very embarrassed.

Why I am telling you, my dear reader, about all I went through in such detail? I want you to be sure that our God is the only Living God. God is mighty and can bring you back and restore you from your deepest pit—regardless of how deep it is. He can bring you back from any fire, regardless of how big it is, any valley of grief or mourning or sorrow—even if the mountain is higher than the clouds in the sky. Though your reflection may be telling you a different message, train yourself to trust more in God's promises. His Word is reality—even if it is not visible now in your life and your body.

> Now Faith is the substance of things hoped for, the evidence of things not seen. (Hebrews 11:1 KJV)

> Heaven and earth will pass away, but my words will not pass away. (Luke 21:33 KJV)

In bed, I did not worry too much or think about my condition. The morphine IV was constantly dripping narcotics into my veins, but I was listening to the people in my room. All of my neighbors had different health issues, but all of us were in critical situation. Most people were facing different types of cancer, taking chemo, or living their final months on earth. They often had family members sitting with them and talking with them. After several hours, I was aware of everyone's story. Their stories did not bring me much hope, but I soon fell asleep, which was very good.

I was quite weak because of the surgery and fasting before and after surgery. A day later, I was transferred from the intensive care unit to a regular hospital room because they needed a bed for someone else. They moved me to a room that was close to the nurse's station for the rest of my days in the hospital, which had some cons and pros. The benefits were that the nurses visited me more often, but it was noisy when they were chatting, especially when the shifts were changing and there were twice as many people as usual. When new a team came in, they were loudly sharing news, jokes, and how they spent their weekends. These normal life events continued for them—but not for me or those with me in the hospital.

The whole world was divided into a world inside and outside of the hospital. For me, it was the hospital world every day. The nurses and patients sometimes shared things from their personal lives.

After a couple of days, I started slowly walking in the hospital corridor. Taking several steps was a big improvement for me. One of the nurses from the intensive care unit helped me walk slowly around the department. We had several stops, and I would sit down to rest. Those first small steps into my new life required boldness and strength. Skinny and weak, I was not sure if I could do it without help and support. I asked the nurse if she could hold my elbow, but she said, "Do it by yourself. I will be beside you, and I will not let you fall down."

I kept one hand on the portable IV stand. I wore a hospital robe and focused on accomplishing my goal. I did not pay attention to my appearance. My hair had not been washed since my surgery, and I did not even bother to comb it. As we were walking, I shared a story from the book I had read many years ago. An Asian king was very sick, and there didn't seem to be any remedy that could help him. He beheaded many doctors after their unsuccessful attempts to heal him. The almighty king was paralyzed and bedridden. He promised to give half of his kingdom to anyone who could help him.

Finally, one man said, "I can do it with only one condition: no security can be in the room or beside the door when I am with the king. Even if the king calls for security, no one is allowed to disturb us."

The king agreed to meet any conditions in order walk again.

The healer closed the door to the king's bedroom and said, "Stand and walk."

The king tried, but he could not stand. After several attempts, the weary and hopeless king fell on the pillows.

The healer opened his pants and started to pee on the face of his king.

The king's blood boiled, and he was furious. He called the soldiers, but no one came because of his command to not disturb them for any reason when the healer was in his bedroom. The king lifted his body to try to reach the healer, but he could not catch him. The doctor was peeing and laughing right in the king's face. The king collected all the force that was in him to reach the offender and finally took a first step and a second step and then started to chase the healer around his bedroom.

I think the Holy Spirit encouraged me through this story, and it had more meaning for me than for her at the time. I laughed with my sweet nurse, a young pretty girl. She was the same one who was very kind to me right after the surgery. She found me even though I was not in the intensive care unit, and she willing to help me learn to walk again. Thank you, God, for your amazing help through the people around me. God bless them all.

After transferring me to a new room, I was told that my surgeon wanted to check my remaining adrenal gland. When you have two adrenal glands, one is sleeping. She wanted to be sure that the remaining gland was functioning properly and producing enough hormones to support my heart and my entire system. They kept the open access to the artery on my neck in case of an emergency. On top of all the IVs with water, liquids, food, and morphine, and my catheter, I had a sexy plastic tube in my neck.

Every day, someone from my family visited me at the hospital. The day I received the news that there was a possibility that my only remaining adrenal gland could go to sleep and not function at all, Andrew and Isadora were visiting me. I was worried about how my gland was working and what would happen if something went wrong. I started to experience heart pain and breathing problems.

My son had no idea what to do, and Isadora tried to hide her worries by moving a bottle around the table with trembling hands. It was a tough time for me and for my kids. They bought a parking pass for the hospital and tried to adjust to their busy lives and the daily hospital visits. My daughter had broken her leg and was attending university with crutches. It was slippery winter weather already, but even that did not stop her from coming to see me.

My son called the nurse, and she took some blood tests. After the necessary analyses, found that it was a panic attack. Fear could produce panic attacks that looked like heart attacks. My adrenal gland was working well. From that day on, I asked my kids to bring me CDs with worship and the New Testament since the Bible was still too heavy for me to lift.

My second room had room for two people. A flat-screen TV was installed close to the ceiling on top of each bed. My nurses encouraged me to watch different channels, but I had no desire to watch any of the programs. Nothing looked important compared to what I was facing. In that condition, I realized how short and precious time is—and you don't know when your time is up.

When I was not sleeping, I read the New Testament. I kept it on my chest on top of my blanket. It was a pocket-size edition from Gideon. After reading a couple of words, I would meditate and repeat them several times until I fell asleep again.

The doctors in the hospital were visiting twice per day: in the morning and in the evening. In addition, some surgical assistants visited me. The middle-aged males were always followed by several medical students from the university. They did checkups in the morning, and I was told that I looked very good for the type of surgery I had undergone. One even said that he had not expected me to recover so fast.

I smiled, pointed to my small New Testament, and said, "God is helping me."

My first roommate in the hospital was about the same age as me. She was in the hospital because of internal bleeding from intestinal cancer. She had gone through several treatments, but she experienced bleeding and was hospitalized. When she was telling me her story, she constantly said, "My cancer." I never did that and kept a biblical passage in my memory.

> Death and life are in the power of the tongue.
> (Proverbs 18:21 KJV)

I found out that her diagnosis was bad, but she was in much better condition physically than I was. She was able to walk and had much more energy than I did. I could only walk with a walker, wires, several IVs, and a catheter. This "little train" followed me each step from the bed to the washroom and to the corridor. Finally, I was able to look at myself without fear when I was washing my face and my body with a wet towel. I was still too weak for a luxury treatment like a shower or a bath. I realized that you need strength and energy to take a shower or a bath.

After a couple of days, my roommate was transferred to a different room. Later that afternoon, I got a new neighbor. He was approximately thirty-five years old, a little overweight, and had red hair and a fashionable beard. He was suffering from a sharp pain and moaned all the time. His moaning reminded me of a thought that came to me out of the blue right after my surgery: "Keep your mouth shut and do not moan." Much later, I realized that if I had moaned, it would have produced thoughts of pity in my mind, and it would have made me weaker than I was. I think the Holy Spirit gave me this knowledge when I moaned after seeing my reflection in the mirror right after the surgery.

I was listening to the moaning of this young man, and he whispered, "Oh, no. Oh."

The nurse came, and my new roommate explained what was happening to him. He was diagnosed with prostate problems and had been hospitalized due to the pain.

The nurse tried to calm him down and offered to let him watch TV, but he said that he didn't have time for that. Neither he nor I were in the mood to watch meaningless shows compared to what we were dealing with at that moment. We were facing a life-and-death situation, and it could be the end. *Is this it? Is this the end?* I do not know what his answer was to these same thoughts, but I had only one answer from God's promises in the Bible. Some of the promises I memorized, and some I kept reading between my naps. I was constantly on morphine, and other IVs provided my only meals.

> Wherefore take unto you the whole armor of God,
> that ye may be able to withstand in the evil day, and
> having done all, to stand. (Ephesians 6:13 KJV)

The surgeon came to see my new neighbor and said that they wanted to perform surgery that night. The man needed to avoid any meals during the preparation processes.

The doctor started to discuss all the details of the surgery.

From the moment I got this guy as my roommate, the whole atmosphere in the room changed dramatically. From the general talk about life and health with my previous roommate, it turned to constant crying and moaning, and I was still dealing with my own fear. In fact, when the surgeon was talking about all the details and the possibility of spreading of the cancer, I felt a deep desire to focus on the Bible. I was holding onto my faith, and I focused on God for my healing because the cold hands of fear started to crush me when the doctor discussed the possibility of the cancer growing inside my body. I could not leave the room because I had just done my walk in the corridor. I simply did not have the energy to walk away at that time. I started to plug my ears with earplugs.

I was hopeless, and the fear was rising inside of me because of what I was hearing. I started to feel another panic attack coming on.

The doctor looked at me and saw that I was fighting against my own fear. He said, "We can discuss the rest a little later."

For several hours, I was asleep. I woke up in the middle of night when the staff took my neighbor for surgery. The nurse was telling him that he would be back in the same room after the surgery, and that was why they were leaving his slippers and clothes. When I woke up, his things were still there, right beside his bed, but he never came back.

A little later, a man from the hospital with a bunch of paper came to the room to pick up his things. He told me that my roommate had died during his surgery.

> You do not know what tomorrow will bring. What is your life? You are a mist that appears for a little while and then vanishes. (James 4:14 ISV)

Dear Reader, if you have not accepted Jesus as your Savior, please stop reading this and pray. Say this prayer out loud right now:

> Dear God, I want to be a part of Your family. You said in Your Word that if I acknowledge that You raised Jesus from the dead, and that I accept Him as my Lord and Savior, I would be saved. So, God, I now say that I believe You raised Jesus from the dead and that He is alive and well. I accept Him now as my personal Lord and Savior. I accept my salvation from sin right now. I am now saved. Jesus is my Lord. Jesus is my Savior. Thank You, Father God, for forgiving me, saving me, and giving me eternal life with You. Amen.

In the hospital, life in general was in a completely different rhythm and measure compared to the world outside of the hospital. An invisible war was present constantly. The battles were critical, and some of solders were leaving the battlefield.

My third roommate had a problem with his gallbladder. He was an eighty-five-year-old farmer from a small community near Calgary. He could easily have been a handsome, powerful, and successful businessman in past, but now he was a broken old man who was fighting with pain and fear. He was completely hopeless—maybe for the first time in his life.

The truth is that sometimes we plan, schedule, and set goals, but tomorrow is only in God's hands.

I was freed from the catheter and the liquid and food IVs. I was familiar with how to start eating properly again because I used to fast for spiritual and physical cleansing purposes more than ten years ago. After trying sweet pudding and jelly from the hospital menu, which the dietitian suggested, I asked my family to bring me organic, unsweetened apple and pumpkin pudding for kids from the grocery store.

Slowly but surely, I was doing my walking several times per day. I was walking and listening to the worship with my headset and filling myself with songs of my dearest Jesus. Each step and each day in there gave me healing strength and energy.

My daughter-in-law brought me an iPod Shuffle, a tiny weightless square that I could easily carry when I was walking. I still had my pocket-sized New Testament. I kept it on my chest and constantly read it when I was awake. With prayers from my family and friends, I was well equipped. I was very optimistic, and when I walked, I was not alone anymore. God was with me. The rest was from Him—from my dearest Jesus. I realized that I was not keeping my back straight, but I stopped myself in the middle of my routine of walking in the corridor of the hospital.

I am writing this book about something that happened almost five years ago. I would compare the time in the hospital—before and after my surgery—to a war where soldiers are facing battles every day. The result of the battles usually depends on the strategy of the plan, how well the soldier is trained, and the size and the strength of the army standing behind you when you are attacking the enemies or the enemies are attacking you. To claim victory, you need to build a smart and active attack and have a strong defense.

As I was walking along the corridor, I saw a young Indian guy.

He was sitting on his bed and vomiting. Noise from his room caught my attention, and I looked through the open door. A nurse held a pot on one side of his bed, and the doctor was on another side. They were both trying to comfort him and help him get through his difficult time. He was sixteen or eighteen years old and tall and looked nice. His big black eyes were looking around with hope and fear.

For a moment, our eyes met. I felt a connection through his eyes. I saw struggle and horror. I will never forget his big expressive eyes. "Can anyone save me?" He was scared to death and moaning. I recognized him. I had seen him from a distance. Several times, I saw him in the corridor. He was walking as slowly as I did. We were both were carrying a bunch of wires and our IVs.

I could not keep my tears away and walked back to my room. As I was passing the nursing station, I heard that he was suffering from the final stages of stomach cancer. One of the young nurses said, "I really hope he does not die on my shift tonight."

The next day, his dad and my surgeon passed me as I was walking in the corridor. The dad was saying that his son felt better, but the doctor did not look optimistic. Unfortunately, her facial expression was not promising, but she did not say anything and respected the dad's feelings.

My first roommate saw me walking with headphones in my ears. I was learning to keep my back straight, my hair was combed, and I had fewer wires behind me. I had no catheter or morphine IV. The water and liquid meals were behind me. I was still weak—after seven days without eating, my muscles had disappeared—but something inside of me was telling me I would be fine.

She stopped me, and we sat down on some chairs to chat. She said, "It is amazing how you've improved. I look at you and think it is a clear sign that you have a chance to live."

I said, "This is my God, and only He gives me strength in addition to my family and friends. Worship and His Word give me life. I only have hope in Him." I asked her about her beliefs, and she said that she believed in miracles from God. She was listening to me with interest, but I could easily read her eyes: "It sounds great, but it's hard to believe."

It is not about understanding. It is about trust—trust in Him. We all are learning to trust in our God and His promises more and more. I had more levels of faith to learn and more difficulties to overcome to return to a normal life, but I did not know it at that time. Thank You, God, for that.

My life journey was continuing, and I was still breathing.

CHAPTER 10

Home Sweet Home

I was dreaming about being at home again, and I sincerely believed I would feel much better there. Many people have the same feeling in life-and-death situations because they were happy and healthy at home. In Ukraine, people say, "When you are at home, even the walls can help."

After many years walking with Lord, I can add, "Walls can help if you have the Word of God on them."

In addition to being at home again and in a safe environment with my family, having the Word of God is crucial for achieving the victory and continuing in victory.

As I entered the house for the first time after the surgery, my daughter said, "Now you do not need these papers with the words from the Bible on our kitchen cabinet doors. You already passed the surgery, right?"

Something inside of me made me say, "No." I needed them even more than before the surgery because I was facing emotional and physical restoration. I had no idea what kind of battle would be in front of me—and neither did my daughter. Only the Holy

Spirit—the precious gift of love from God who keeps and sustains my tomorrow in His mighty hands—was aware of my future. No one, not even my close family members, was able to be with me 24/7, read my thoughts, and give me knowledge, strength, and peace. When everyone left the house or had other responsibilities, I only had one precious Companion. It had been years and years since I accepted Jesus, and I had my personal time with Him. He was always available and ready to be with me.

Life can be overwhelming. We are living in technologically advanced time, and there can be an overload of information, news, and events in our personal lives and in the world. The most precious thing we have is our time.

Dearest readers, please make time for personal and intimate time with the Holy Spirit. This delightful friendship will save your life someday. It will lead you out of total defeat with whatever you struggle with. It will lead you to total healing, restoration, and victory. Our supernatural Lord has no limits—only we, as humans, have limits—and we can only limit Him if we do not make it a priority to grow ourselves with Him.

> You, Lord, are my lamp;
> the Lord turns my darkness into light.
> With your help I can advance against a troop;
> with my God I can scale a wall.
> As for God, his way is perfect:
> The Lord's word is flawless;
> he shields all who take refuge in him.
> For who is God besides the Lord?
> And who is the Rock except our God?
> It is God who arms me with strength
> and keeps my way secure.
> He makes my feet like the feet of a deer;
> he causes me to stand on the heights.
> He trains my hands for battle;

my arms can bend a bow of bronze.
You make your saving help my shield;
your help has made[c] me great.
You provide a broad path for my feet,
so that my ankles do not give way.
(2 Samuel 22:29–37 NIV)

From the moment I opened the front door of my home after the hospital and celebrated my way back to life with having a pedicure that my daughter offered on my skinny legs, certain thoughts were torturing my mind. I was physically wounded and had a large scar from my chest to the very bottom of my body. All my clothes were too big on me, and I went from size large to size small. Even my shoes were too big, especially boots. My reflection in the mirror showed me only a shadow of the beauty I once had. Every time I saw myself, I said, "For we walk by faith, not by sight" (2 Corinthians 5:7 KJV).

It was winter, and the snow and ice on the road were not the best for me after surgery. I had to walk around my own home to exercise, change the scenery, and meditate on the Word of God outside of my home. I was not even able to lift a small pot with soup to heat it for my lunch. I was physically weak, and I was trapped in my own home. I only had God and His Word to defend me from Satan's attacks. Most of the time, I was alone because my kids were full-time students at the university. My son was married and lived in a different part of the city. Right after surgery, my husband went abroad on a business trip.

Most of the time, I was alone with my Lord. As soon I had pitying thoughts in my brain, my back would hunch over again. My hands would tremble, and it scared my daughter when she saw me after school. She remembered me as being full of energy and a hard worker around the home, in the kitchen, and in the garden since her childhood.

I was wounded emotionally because of the memories I had.

Different pictures swarmed in my memory. It would start in the morning, right when I opened my eyes, and the memories would come back to me at night: the Arabic hospital, ambulances, diagnostics, daily nauseas, surgery, the hospital in Calgary, and the faces of dying people. I needed time and effort to grow up in the faith with my God and His supernatural nature for a full healing and restoration.

> For I will restore health unto thee, and I will heal
> thee of thy wounds, saith the Lord. (Jeremiah 30:17
> KJV)

The very next day at home, I experienced one of the attacks. I ran to the only remedy I was aware of and that always worked well: worshipping my God. I turned on the disc with my favorite worship of Benny Hinn's ministry, lifted my hands, and started slowly moving in my living room. I was pretending that I was dancing for my Lord.

At that moment, all of my being divided into two parts: my wounded, weak flesh and the spirit that dwells in me. I instantly cleaved to my Lord. Heavy tears from my wounded soul covered my cheeks and neck. The grief, pain, bitterness, and fear splashed out of my soul, cleaning myself deeper and deeper. It was something that was only between Jesus and me.

My daughter was studying upstairs in her room with her door closed. Several years later, she said, "I saw you, Mom, when you were lifting up your hands in our living room right after the hospital."

Life continued, and all of my family members made choices that formed their life paths. My husband left after several days because of his business trip abroad. I was looking at how quickly and joyfully he was packing his stuff. I thought he must be excited to be free and that he was probably tired of me now—or what was left of me. I did not tell anyone about those thoughts.

The thoughts had no proof, and the thoughts were leading me

to the next step of growing myself in my faith and strength. My second book will be about helping women and men overcome the betrayal of their spouses in the middle of fighting for their lives or in the middle of any crisis. My life passed with my dearest Teacher. The Holy Spirit gave me a wish to share with my brothers and sisters a delightful testimony of how our Father protects us. His help turns our grief into blessings.

Time flies, as we know. After a couple weeks, the biopsy results from the eight-centimeter tumor were sent back. I was invited to see my surgeon for the first time after the surgery. It was not an easy visit for me. I would be going back to the place where there were the most painful memories that I was trying to forget. Before entering the hospital, I saw many patients in hospital robes, and some of them were carrying walkers with IVs and oxygen.

The Foothills Hospital had a long line for the receptionist. To try to avoid negative thoughts and to change the picture in front of my eyes, I went to the gift shop. It was almost empty in the middle of the weekday, and I exhaled a sigh of relief. I focused my attention on small, cute gifts and tried to think positive and encouraging thoughts.

While I was looking at the little angels and other small gifts, I heard a woman talking loudly on her cell phone. She was describing her husband's brain tumor in detail. All her suspicions, worries, grief, and stress were exactly what I was trying to get rid of in my own life. I left the gift shop and soon was sitting in the doctor's room with my son.

My surgeon came back and said that the tumor had cancerous cells—but they were not sure about exactly what it was because there were not many studies about adrenal cancer. She wanted to refer me to Tom Baker Hall, which was located in the same hospital. It was a place for following up with cancer patients.

I was claiming and lifting my trust that I was healed. I was reading Psalm 91, thinking about a long life, and never accepting the cancer or saying "my cancer." My brain was rejecting any possibility of being with other cancer patients, but my doctor said that was the policy for any postsurgical patients with a health history like mine. She had to refer me there. It reminded me of my prayer when I asked God to show me that He could heal even what doctors can't heal. Even after doing all the scans, she said the organs were too close to the tumor to guarantee that no organs would be damaged. She might need to cut the liver or another organ. The liver can be damaged in such a way that surgery can't do anything. The surgery was scheduled for six hours, but God changed it to two and a half hours—and all my organs were healthy and clean.

I appreciated all the help from the doctors, but I was keeping in mind that the last word is from God—even it's only official policy. My Banker Hall appointment was booked, and as soon I came through the door, I found another clinic inside the hospital. They had different receptionists, files, and oncologists. The patients had family members or close friends to support them. Most of the patients were weak, some of them were bald, and some were barely walking with walkers. Most of them had pale faces. It was a living cemetery, and I made a decision to refuse to belong to it because of what God had promised me. My eyes were reflecting all the horror of what I was seeing, and I opened my new Testament:

> Whoever dwells in the shelter of the Most High will rest in the shadow of the Almighty.
>
> I will say of the Lord, "He is my refuge and my fortress, my God, in whom I trust."
>
> Surely he will save you from the fowler's snare and from the deadly pestilence.
>
> He will cover you with his feathers, and under his wings you will find refuge; his faithfulness will be your shield and rampart. You will not fear the terror of night, nor the arrow that flies by day, nor the pestilence that stalks in the darkness, nor the plague that destroys at midday. A thousand may fall

at your side, ten thousand at your right hand, but it
will not come near you. You will only observe with
your eyes and see the punishment of the wicked.
(Psalm 91:1–8 NIV)

Whosoever shall seek to save his life shall lose it;
and whosoever shall lose his life shall preserve it.
(Luke 17:33 KJV)

Right across from receptionist, there was a big room with
several beds. The curtains were opened, and I could see a middle-
aged man on the bed. He was trembling and moaning loudly. His
son was in his thirties and held his hand. I could easily read the
unbearable grief on his face.

When I went in with my son and husband, the receptionist
opened the file and referred me to another desk. I got an identification
card with a number, and when I asked what it was about, they said,
"It is for the rest of your life."

I looked at the card, gave it to my son, and said, "I do not want
to keep it."

After several minutes of waiting for the oncologist, they
called my name. A well-trained nurse asked me several questions.
A handsome doctor came in next. He was my age, and he went
through all the information after my surgery and tried to convince
me to have chemotherapy in case the cancer came back. He was
sitting very close to me and looking at me with interest.

My legs were much too skinny for my winter boots. All his talk
was like a kick to the bottom of my stomach.

He said, "We did the most effective treatment, which was
surgery, but we will not be able to do it a second time. Chemotherapy
is a good option to prevent the spread of cancer through the blood."
He was looking right into my eyes.

I thought for several seconds. My family was silent. It was a moment for my personal decision—only mine. I took all of my strength and said, "No."

To say no, it took all of my boldness and faith that I had. I knew that chemo would damage my immune system, but I left it as it was and trusted in God's promise. When I signed the paper, he said, "We just tried to gather information around your cases. We know how to treat breast cancer, but there's no data for treating adrenal glands. I have only one patient who tried to do chemo in your condition, and she dropped out of chemo after several days because of the side effects."

I said, "I know about it, and I choose to trust my God."

For you, dear reader, it could be a different choice, but for me, it was what I felt at that moment.

One of these visits caused me stress for several days, and I was using all-natural remedies (see "My Holistic Approach" chapter). Nothing worked well without prayer and reading the Bible, several times a day as much as I needed.

> So, then faith comes by hearing, and hearing by the
> Word of God. (Romans 10:17 KJV)

After surgery, it was a very difficult time—not only because of the memories about my own disease but also because people were suffering and dying in front of my eyes in the hospital and in my room. At home, I was spending all of my time with prayers, reading the Bible, watching DVDs with preaching, or listening to CDs with worship and preaching. I tried to keep myself busy as much as my physical strength allowed. I was slow, but my muscles were getting stronger. Every morning, I was claiming God's promises about health and longevity. I was trying to do small chores; every day, I was slowly improving my tiny activities, but I was still not able to lift a pot with soup and walk around home without resting.

The most difficult part was healing the emotional wounds. I was cutting veggies on a cutting board, and thoughts from the past came across my mind again and tortured my mind. Satan whispered the paraphrase that I know from my childhood right into my ears: "The past will never change." This sentence gave me the thought that I will always suffer with my memory.

I was alone in a big house, and only the Holy Spirit was with me all the time. I dropped the knife, fell down on my knees in the kitchen, and cried in desperation to God: "Please, help me forget the past. Please erase it from my memory. Only You can do it—no one else."

My tears covered my face, and the knowledge from the Holy Spirit came in the middle of darkness to light up my entire being: "Do you think the past is permanent? My Word is permanent." His light was converted into God's Holy Words in my brain.

Yes. that's right. If God's Word was not permanent, God would not have built heaven and earth with His Word, Lazarus would not have been resurrected after three days of being dead, and the blind man would not have regained his sight. The blind man and the bleeding woman would never have been healed. All of them had lost their health, but God's Word changed the past.

> Then they took away the stone from the place where the dead was laid. And Jesus lifted up his eyes, and said, "Father, I thank thee that thou hast heard me.
>
> "And I knew that thou hearest me always: but because of the people which stand by I said it, that they may believe that thou hast sent me.
>
> "And when he thus had spoken, he cried with a loud voice, Lazarus, come forth." (John 11:41–43 KJV)

The Bible is full of examples of the Word of God changing conditions that occurred in the past. I do not believe in the parable that I heard in my childhood:

> Thus have ye made the commandment of God of
> none effect by your tradition. (Matthew 15:6 NIV)

After this answer from God, my mood turned from depression to victory.

It is always happening with me when God talks. He will never put you down—even from the deepest pit of sorrow, anxiety, or fear. He will lift you up in one second with His gentle touch. It's the most effective 911 call that I know. I found myself staying on the rock of His Word again. Satan was defeated.

The tears of joy and adoration of my God—who is always beautiful, holy, almighty, and loving—were washing and cleaning my heart again and again and leading me toward His call.

This is one of example of the daily battles I was facing. These battles and victories had grown me spiritually—much faster than any preaching, conferences, or online Bible courses. It was my personal intimate experience with my Only Living God, and I was getting know Him more and since I fell in love with Him in 1994.

After several months, I asked my surgeon to do a checkup with me instead of the oncologist at Banker Hall. I also asked for an MRI instead of a City Scan to avoid radiation. She agreed to follow up with me until my results were good.

Thank You, God, for Your Faithfulness. Since my surgery, my results are normal—and the surgeon never invited me to her office. She was busy with sick patients, and she had several years of people in line for surgery. God gave me a very talented doctor.

Slowly but surely, my strength, memory, and writing skills returned. I tried to write and found that my handwriting ability was gone. I was learning to write again, but I still had no clue why it happened with me. Only God knows, and the most important part is that He restored it.

I have a longtime connection with several ministries: Benny Hinn, Morris Cerullo, and Reinhard Bonnke. The summer after my surgery, I went to Morris Cerullo's International Conference in San

Diego. They gave their partners a big discount for accommodations, and I was thirsty for more presence of the Holy Spirit in my life. I begged my husband to fly, and my daughter agreed to fly with us.

It was June 2014, and summer had just begun in Calgary. San Diego was already hot enough to burn my skin. The flight was short and joyful in expectation of the divine atmosphere of holy presence and revelations from the living Word of God. The three-day conference was located in a cute country hotel with small cottages, an outdoor pool, a garden, and cozy restaurants. The rainbow of colorful roses attracted my attention and made me feel like I was at home. Many people from different countries came for the intensive training, and we had daily prayers at six o'clock in the morning. The children of God worshipped His beauty and expressed our love for the Lord.

It was mostly pastors and leaders of ministries. There were several worshipping groups from different countries and very well-known preachers from the United States, Africa, and Israel. After the morning prayer and breakfast, we had a of conference until lunchtime. That evening, the teaching and worshipping continued until suppertime. My daughter made a decision to fly back earlier, and my husband drove her to the airport for the afternoon flight.

On the second day, after morning preaching, I came across a Chinese woman who was pushing a wheelchair with a paralyzed middle-aged man. The man caught my attention because the bottom part of his face was paralyzed. His face was pale and skinny, his hands were deformed, and he had been sitting in the chair for a long time.

I opened the door and held it open for the couple, and the man reminded me of my dad who was paralyzed for six months when he was fighting dementia. My heart turned toward this man, and I heard God's words: "Pray for him." This thought flashed in my mind totally unexpectedly and shocked me. Besides all the important people around who were there with their churches and ministries, I was a small, thirsty-for-God woman who had just gone through major surgery. I was feeling like Cinderella at a big ball in the presence of His Majesty, our Almighty and Loving God.

Why me? Yes, I will pray about this man and lift a prayer in my hotel room. God told me that He wanted me to stop them and pray loudly right there and right then.

Several men in expensive suits passed us with usual greetings, and I was still fighting with my thoughts, like Moses, when he was saying that no one would listen to him in Egypt if he went back to talk to the Jews.

Several minutes later, this couple crossed the small plaza to my hotel room. I was thinking about how it would look if I stopped them. I was a small Cinderella from nowhere around these big presentable people and their mighty appearances. An international conference was a routine part of their lifestyle and part of their job description. Many of them already recognized each other. They had connections and were talking loudly right beside us. They did not hear the word that God said to me. Why? I was really confused.

I was walking and praying silently—even though I perfectly understood that it was not what God wanted from me. The man looked like a living corpse. He was skinny, pale, paralyzed, and deformed. Saliva was falling on his bib from a slightly opened mouth.

The couple turned in a different direction. It was a hot summer in San Diego. The heat had already risen, and on my way back to my hotel room, I saw children screaming wildly and enjoying refreshments by the pool. The colorful flowers radiated an amazing smell, and tireless hummingbirds were in the middle of their business.

On my way back to my hotel room, I was thinking about what God had said to me. It was something totally new in my personal experience of walking with Him. I had prayed many times for sick people in the church back in Ukraine and in prayer groups in Calgary. I prayed for people's needs when I was strong and healthy and when I got authority from the pastor. Now it was different. I was still physically not strong and very skinny. In fact, I spent a lot of time with my daughter looking for a swimsuit to hide my bones. It was a public place—the middle of a plaza—and important people from the ministry were around. It was something I had to learn from God, and it paralyzed me on my way back to my room.

I tried to clarify His will on my life and study Him more. Holding the picture of the couple in my mind, I asked, "Really? You want *me* to pray for sick people?" In that second goose bumps, like a fresh breeze, covered me from top to bottom. Still not believing it, I asked the question a second time—and the same goose bumps covered me. At that moment, the temperature outside was more than ninety degrees. It was definitely not a cold wind.

Being in shock from the discovery of what God wanted me to do in my life—and still not understanding why He picked me—I found myself in my hotel room. I dropped to my knees to worship and pray to God with my tears, adoration, and love for seeing me as His vessel undeservingly.

Soon after my husband came back from the airport, I shared how God revealed His will and how I was scared to pray loudly for the paralyzed man in the middle of the plaza.

The next day was Pentecostal Day and the last day of the conference. From the very morning, a divine presence of God was in the conference room. The people around me were passionately worshipping God. A group from Israel opened the worship, and anointing was descending as the first words were sung. The Holy Spirit filled me so abundantly with His joy and presence that I could not stand calmly. I was overflowing with the Holy Spirit's presence, and my legs jumped and danced to express my love and admiration of my Lord. I forgot where I was and who was around me. The fire of love for He who is so real, alive, merciful, and holy embraced all of me.

I doubted for a second, and then I shut off my brain and thoughts about what people would think about me. No one danced at that moment even though the worship was full of joy and applause. I was rendered on the crest of the wave of the Holy Spirit, and I danced as though it was the last dance in my life. I was in full adoration and love of His Majesty. After my dance, a woman asked if I was a Jew because I danced like Jewish people danced. I smiled at her and answered, "Only spiritually."

Morris Cerullo was speaking and praying each day of the conference, and he went to the platform and said that he wanted to preach about something, but God spoke to him and said that he needed to say something else.

> Surely the Lord GOD will do nothing, but he
> revealeth his secret unto his servants the prophets.
> (Amos 3:7 KJV)

The Word of God talks about the fear that bound his children. Fear was an obstacle to victory. These words were full of love and encouragement from the Father who cares for His kids. He cares for and leads them from lesson to lesson, from step to step, and from failure to victory.

As soon these words touched my ears, it struck my heart. I was feeling like a loser because of my fear about praying in public. Tears of appreciation filled my eyes. How real is it that our Holy Spirit is so close to us? It always blows my mind.

Several preachers were sharing revelations from the Word of God after worshipping, and I was writing notes and trying to reflect on places where the Holy Spirit highlighted my heart. After the lunch break, we had opportunities to buy books, CDs, and DVDs with anointed preaching and worshipping. I met people from different parts of world. I met people who loved God and gathered together in San Diego for the International Conference with Morris Cerullo.

The last day was almost gone, and before closing, we were all worshipping the Lord. Morris Cerullo was leading the last minutes of the conference. People were standing and worshipping God in the atmosphere of unity with the Holy Spirit. I felt undeniable joy and like I was in the right place at the right time. The Lord wanted to see me working with the hearts of His children.

I noticed somebody running down the front rows beside the stage. All of my attention was on worshipping the Lord and my spirit. I guess I was experiencing heavenly joy. Finally, I asked my husband who was standing beside me. Maybe someone from the ministry was in a rush to grab something. The crowd, the music, and the special atmosphere made it hard to understand and see what was going on in front.

Morris Cerullo and his prayer team were praying for sick people, and I was told that someone in a wheelchair had been touched by the Holy Spirit. He was healed instantly, and he was running around the conference room.

As soon as I heard those words, I thought it could be the man I saw yesterday. At the end of the service, I was running through the crowd and toward the stage. I saw a group of people standing around someone who was on the floor right in front of the stage. Some of the people were praying, and some of them were just watching what was going on. When I was close enough to recognize who was on the floor, I saw it was the man who God told me to pray for. A hopelessly paralyzed man with deformed legs and hands—who was not able to keep his saliva or eat properly without the bib—was touched by mighty and gentle Holy Spirit and was running around the conference room.

Tears were pouring down my face like heavy rain. I whispered, "O, Lord, You are beautiful and holy. Forgive me, Lord." I was whispering again and again without being able to stop myself. I was overwhelmed by what I had seen and what I had learned about my dearest Healer. God is alive!

I was not able to look away from this blond, skinny middle-aged man who was on the floor under the power of the Holy Spirit. He looked like he was on an operating table. It reminded me of when I was in the Foothills Hospital in Calgary. This lucky man had major surgery performed by the most talented Surgeon in the universe:

the Holy Spirit. I stood there for a while, and my husband dragged me away from the crowd. "Let's go." My legs slowly followed him. I was still under the influence of what I had seen.

We stopped beside the place where people were selling Christian materials, and I decided what I should get. As soon as we walked closer to the exit, the Holy Spirit told me to go back and watch the man again. I took several steps toward the exit and was ready to open the door.

The Holy Spirit said, "Go back." There was something that God wanted to show me.

My husband did not get the point of going back. "What we are going to do in an empty conference room?"

It had already been more than an hour since the conference finished, and even the musicians and people from the ministry were leaving. At that moment, I could not answer why we needed to go back. I just said that I didn't know why. I only knew what the Holy Spirit was telling me. Finally, he agreed, and we opened the door again.

The room was almost empty, and there was no one on the stage. I searched the room and found a couple of people who were sitting and talking. The light was not too bright. In the last row of seats, I saw a couple and walked up to them. As I was walking toward them, I realized that it was the couple who God showed me yesterday when He told me to pray for his healing. I was very surprised to see them there. *Why are they still here? What is going on?* I rushed across the hall to find out the answer.

There was no wheelchair at that time, and the man was sitting in one of the seats. His wife was holding small bags with water bottles, snacks, and bibs. The middle-aged Asian woman was not too tall and not too small. She had short black hair, and her clothes were simple, calming, and neat. She was standing beside her husband with no idea what she needed to do. At the moment, I did not see any panic in her eyes. I started to talk to her to try to figure out what the problem was, and she told me the whole story of what happened with her husband.

Her husband had been paralyzed since childhood and even had mental problems; sometimes his mind was not very clear. When she married him, she started to pray for him and go to prayer groups. She also was regularly reading the Bible to him. After a while, her husband's mind was healed completely.

The day I saw him, I did not notice any signs of mental problems. He was speaking slowly, like a person who is in deep thought, but his answers were totally appropriate and normal. God answered her wish to bring her husband to the conference, and during the service on Pentecostal Day, the Holy Spirit touched her husband. He suddenly jumped up from the wheelchair and started to run down the long hall. I saw him running in front of the stage.

After several cycles of running, he fell into the nearest seat. He repeated his running after the service was finished. The man simply could not walk. He needed to learn it slowly and trust that the same God who healed him—and gave ability to run for the first time in his life—would give him the strength to walk slowly. It was something I had never thought about before. Interesting.

I turned to the man and introduced myself. He was totally confused and overwhelmed because of what had just happened to him. His eyes were open, his hands were shaking, and he looked afraid—but his hands and legs were in perfect shape. I clearly remembered how deformed his hands and legs were.

When I realized that he was in fear because he did not understand what he needed to do now, I recognized the same spirit that was torturing me before and after surgery. As soon as I got this understanding, resentment and anger against Satan filled my heart. I looked in his eyes calmly and confidently and began to pray. I claimed the Word of God over my brother, bound the spirit of fear, and commanded him to leave this man. I shared the story of my healing miracle from a very rare type of cancer and how God was strengthening my faith for several months before I was diagnosed.

He gave me vision and words. I told him that God had a plan for total restoration and a healing miracle. "He told me about his plan to heal you one day ago, but I was not faithful. He was—and is—always!

The man jumped up, energized by power of electricity, and ran. I ran after him, clapping and yelling, "You can do it!"

I felt joyous about the discovery of something overwhelming about the Living God. He is always alive and faithful. It was overflowing in me. When the man fell down on one of the seats again, I stopped beside him. He ran faster than I did, and I could not catch him. His hands were not shaking anymore, and I continued praying for him.

After several minutes, a beautiful African American woman joined us. She shared her healing story from cancer and encouraged the man. I was listening to her and thinking that I never assumed that this small and tender young woman had gone through several life-threatening situations. These battles made her strong and ready to contribute her stories to encourage other people. As we were praying for the man, he jumped up again and ran so fast that I could not catch him.

After a while, we left the conference room, but this experience of touching God's miracle in my life and the life in other people made me a different person. What a privilege to find yourself in God's merciful and loving hands! All the glory goes to Him.

On the airplane, I told my husband that I had bought all the books that I had been dreaming about except one. I wanted to buy the book about Kathryn Kuhlman. When we landed and opened our door, I found a small package from Morris Cerullo Ministry. I did not request anything and was very curious about what was inside. Guess what I found inside the package? It was the book I wanted but did not buy at the conference. It was the book about Kathryn Kuhlman.

> And it shall come to pass, that before they call, I will answer; and while they are yet speaking, I will hear. (Isaiah 65:24 KJV)

CHAPTER 11

My Holistic Approach to Physical and Emotional Restoration

Do you not know that your bodies are temples
of the Holy Spirit, who is in you, whom you have
received from God? You are not your own.
—1 Corinthians 6:19

Most of the time, when people hear this Bible passage, they are only thinking about the spiritual, moral, and emotional aspects. For me, it was a clear reminder that I still live in flesh on this earth and need to take care of my body.

I put my personal time with God in first place and consider it the primary food for my spiritual and emotional health. During my nutrition education, I learned to not ignore my secondary food, which comes from healthy choices, daily meals, and vitamins and minerals. That definitely played and plays a crucial role in my life for physical health besides physical activities and exercises.

Many years ago, these thoughts led me to the Global College of Natural Medicine. After college graduation, I went to the

Institute for Integrative Nutrition, and I learned how to nourish and rejuvenate myself. I decided to adjust the balance in my life for health and longevity.

I graduated from the Global College of Natural Medicine and received a nutritional consultant certificate. In college, I learned subjects that could change life, including anatomy and physiology, toxicity and detoxification, dietary guidelines and physical fitness, orthomolecular nutrition, alternative healing methods, weight loss, and much more.

A passion for natural healing motivated me to continuously upgrade my knowledge of alternative healing and rejuvenation. This passion led me to be a holistic health coach. As a drugless practitioner, I assist my clients with smooth transitions toward reaching their health and longevity goals.

I received my training as a health coach from the Institute for Integrative Nutrition's cutting-edge Health Coach Training Program.

During my training, I studied more than. One hundred dietary theories, practical lifestyle management techniques, and innovative coaching methods with some of the world's top health and wellness experts. My teachers included Dr. Andrew Weil, director of the Arizona Center for Integrative Medicine, Dr. Deepak Chopra, a leader in the field of mind-body medicine, Dr. David Katz, director of Yale University's Prevention Research Center, Dr. Walter Willett, chair of nutrition at Harvard University, Geneen Roth, a bestselling author and an expert on emotional eating, and many other leading researchers and nutrition authorities.

The most important thing my education gave me was the key and direction to help myself and restore my physical body after cancer, overcome middle-age crisis, and support my family and clients.

My transition to healthy living changed me even before I was diagnosed with adrenal gland cancer. I successfully recovered regardless of the conventional medicine that were offered to me at the hospital and when I was at home.

I am certified by the American Association of Drugless Practitioners and am a board-certified holistic health practitioner. I applied what I learned to my life, and it made me look differently inside and outside, and it increased my energy and boosted my immune system.

It's rare for anyone to get an hour to explore their wellness goals with a trained professional. As an integrative nutrition health coach, I can create a supportive environment that enables you to articulate and achieve your goals. Throughout my education, I have been exposed to the most cutting-edge dietary theories and studied highly effective coaching techniques to help you find the right lifestyle that works best for you.

Most approaches to healthy eating dwell on calories, carbohydrates, fats, and proteins. Instead of creating lists of restrictions and good and bad foods, I coach my clients to explore basic improvements and implement gradual changes during our work together. As these pieces accumulate, my clients find the changes collectively create a much larger impact than they originally expected. We work on what you want to improve—within the circumstances of your unique situation.

Could one conversation change your life? Yes. This life-changing holistic program transformed me, and if you are ready to get out of your comfort zone and invest in your health and a successful future, get ready to discover yourself and reach your health goals, rejuvenate your body, and more. Book your free initial consultation for local and long-distance clients at www.lubovhealthylongevity.com.

Before   After

My education has equipped me with extensive knowledge in holistic nutrition, health coaching, and preventive health. I was learning as much as I was practicing. I transformed my favorite recipes, habits, lifestyle and added quality vitamins, minerals, juices, and sprouts, according to my age, my health goals, and the climate where I live. Drawing on these skills and my knowledge of different dietary theories, I work with clients to help them make lifestyle changes that produce real and lasting results.

Some of my friends and family members were skeptical from the very beginning about the changes, but they started noticing that my energy and appearance were changing. I found myself looking younger and slimmer. For years, I spent money on having better hair, better skin, and getting rid of wrinkles. Guess what? Suddenly, after my transition to a healthy lifestyle, I realized that my improved health (better digestion, more energy, better memory, and better sleep) was radiating from inside to outside. The wrinkles around my eyes disappeared, and my hair stopped falling out—even without using the expensive lotion I was addicted to.

This is not just knowledge or business. This is my own life experience for rejuvenating myself in middle age and restoring myself after a life-threatening illness. It was a crucial time for fighting for my life. I am thankful to my Lord. He leads me, and now I can invest, share, and support my best input in my clients' lives.

Client Testimonies

When the doctors diagnosed my mother with breast cancer, I was devastated. I was afraid for my mother, and I was scared about my future. What if I get breast cancer? It was a sudden wakeup call for me to change something in my life to be able to stay healthy and live longer. I immediately booked a one-on-one six-month program with Lubov, and I could not be happier. We meet regularly and address all my concerns and my diet, and we set goals. She brings me samples of products I never knew existed (like kale and quinoa) and recipes to prepare them, and they became part of my daily diet. She gives me tons of useful information. I have noticed the difference in the ways my body is functioning right away. I completely stopped using laxatives, which used to be an integral part my diet. This is something very important to celebrate for someone who struggled with constipation all her life. I am very grateful to Lubov for giving me an opportunity to be a healthier and happier person and for sharing her knowledge with her clients. I highly recommend Lubov to anyone who needs help or improve overall health.

Olga

Your advice to adjust my diet and lifestyle have given me great results so far. Also, because of your professional help, my digestion improved as well. I have more energy. Your suggestions combined with an exercise program have helped me lose fifteen pounds. Thank you very much for taking the time to help me.

Best regards,

Oscar

Hello Lubov,

Because of your professional help and support as a holistic health coach and nutrition consultant, I tremendously increased my immune system by adjusting my diet and lifestyle by adding the necessary supplements. When I got a cold, I was able to overcome my condition after just one day of your treatment. Also, I thank you for improving my digestion system as well.

I am looking forward to working with you,

Alexandra

Lubov is knowledgeable, genuine, and caring. She has helped me make lifestyle changes based on my personal goals. She has impressed upon me the importance of balance in all areas of my life in order to gain control over my eating. Lubov has scientific information regarding all of the food groups, which has led me to an understanding of the nutrients my body requires.

In the relatively short time I have been working with Lubov, I have seen my cravings disappear, I have more energy, and I have started to lose weight.

Barbara

Thank you for all the friendly advice and cooking tips. They have helped me become more cognizant of what I eat and also influenced some of the life choices I make. Your newsletters have reminded me of the importance of physical activities and healthy eating.

Isadora

CHAPTER 12

Healing Words from the Bible

This is the most important chapter in my book, my dearest readers. These are only a few of words of the Book of Life that have given me the ability to breathe when anxiety attacks choked me. They gave me peace when the freezing winds of fear of death embraced me. These words brought me hope when the grief of the reality of my sickness burned my heart and turned me to the joy of victory when Satan whispered hopeless thoughts and bitter tears washed my face and neck.

These promises are only bullets that are killing an enemy in the spiritual war of my life and are reflected on a physical level. I believe it will work for your victory as well—not because of who I am and what I passed or who you are but because of who He is.

These are words from the Holy Bible that the Holy Spirit highlighted for me. I slowly read them several times and digested them until I got spiritual fullness to be strong enough to face the next day. It was important to have daily time with the Holy Spirit. When you have intimate time with God, He will highlight what is best for your condition, situation, and understanding. He is the perfect teacher.

You must rise in Spirit and take authority over your feelings. The Word of God will never change and is necessary for living.

> The spirit of a man will sustain his infirmity; but a wounded spirit who can bear? (Proverbs 18:14 KJV)

> Heaven and earth shall pass away: but my words shall not pass away. (Mark 13:31 KJV)

> Jesus Christ the same yesterday, and today, and forever. (Hebrews 13:8 KJV)

> So shall my word be that goeth forth out of my mouth: it shall not return unto me void, but it shall accomplish that which I please, and it shall prosper in the thing whereto I sent it. (Isaiah 55:11 KJV)

> Even I couldn't see and understand how God will heal me, but I made a choice to give Him all my burns by lifting to Him my prayer and worshipping Him. Trust in the Lord with all thine heart; and lean not unto thine own understanding. In all thy ways acknowledge him, and he shall direct thy paths. (Proverbs 3:5–6 KJV)

> While we look not at the things which are seen, but at the things which are not seen: for the things which are seen are temporal; but the things which are not seen are eternal. (2 Corinthians 4:18 KJV)

Wherefore, sirs, be of good cheer: for I believe God, that it shall be even as it was told me. (Acts 27:25 KJV)

Be not wise in thine own eyes: fear the Lord and depart from evil. It shall be health to thy navel, and marrow to thy bones. (Proverbs 3:7–8 KJV)

And Jesus answered him, saying, It is written, That man shall not live by bread alone, but by every word of God. (Luke 4:4 KJV)

The words I have spoken to you are spirit, and they are life. (John 6:63 KJV)

Casting down arguments and every high thing that exalts itself against the knowledge of God, bringing every thought into captivity to the obedience of Christ. (2 Corinthians 10:5 KJV)

Thou hast made known to me the ways of life; thou shalt make me full of joy with thy countenance. (Acts 2:28 KJV)

I put my trust to Him and He promised me not to be ashamed and be full of joy again. O keep my soul and deliver me: let me not be ashamed; for I put my trust in thee. And shall not God avenge his own elect, which cry day and night unto him, though he bear long with them? (Luke 18:7 KJV)

He sent his word, and healed them, and delivered them from their destructions. (Psalm 107:20 KJV)

For David speaketh concerning him, I foresaw the Lord always before my face, for he is on my right hand, that I should not be moved: Therefore did my heart rejoice, and my tongue was glad; moreover also my flesh shall rest in hope. (Acts 2:25–26 KJV)

Have mercy upon me, O Lord; for I am weak: O Lord, heal me; for my bones are vexed. My soul is also sore vexed: but thou, O Lord, how long?

Return, O Lord, deliver my soul: oh save me for thy mercies' sake. For in death there is no remembrance of thee: in the grave who shall give thee thanks? I am weary with my groaning; all the night make I my bed to swim; I water my couch with my tears. Mine eye is consumed because of grief; it waxeth old because of all mine enemies. Depart from me, all ye workers of iniquity; for the Lord hath heard the voice of my weeping. The Lord hath heard my supplication; the Lord will receive my prayer. (Psalm 6:2–9 KJV)

For whatsoever is born of God overcometh the world: and this is the victory that overcommits the world, even our faith. (1 John 5:4 KJV)

The Lord also will be a refuge[a] for the oppressed, a refuge in times of trouble. And those who know Your name will put their trust in You; For You, Lord, have not forsaken those who seek You. (Psalm 9:9–10 KJV)

If, when evil cometh upon us, as the sword, judgment, or pestilence, or famine, we stand before this house, and in thy presence, (for thy name is in this house) and cry unto thee in our affliction, then thou wilt hear and help.

(2 Chronicles 20:9 KJV)

I keep my faith in Only God who is Alive, who is Supernatural, always in front of me and always Faithful ready to answer. So then faith cometh by hearing, and hearing by the word of God. (Romans 10–17 KJV)

Now faith is the substance of things hoped for, the evidence of things not seen. (Hebrews 11:1 KJV)

Through faith we understand that the worlds were framed by the word of God, so that things which are seen were not made of things which do appear.

(Hebrews 11:3 KJV)

Every good gift and every perfect gift is from above, and cometh down from the Father of lights, with whom is no variableness, neither shadow of turning. (James 1:17 KJV)

Only God can give me peace in the middle of crises, in my fighting for life. Hel leads me through the darkness to Light and Victory. Acquaint now thyself with him and be at peace: thereby good shall come unto thee. (Job 22:21 KJV)

In Him was life, and the life was the light of men. And the light shines in the darkness, and the darkness did not [a]comprehend it. (John 1:4–5 KJV)

Then shall thy light break forth as the morning, and thine health shall spring forth speedily: and thy righteousness shall go before thee; the glory of the Lord shall be thy rearward. (Isaiah 58:8 KJV)

And I say also unto thee, That thou art Peter, and upon this rock I will build my church; and the gates of hell shall not prevail against it.

And I will give unto thee the keys of the kingdom of heaven: and whatsoever thou shalt bind on earth shall be bound in heaven: and whatsoever thou shalt loose on earth shall be loosed in heaven. (Matthew 16:18–19 KJV)

No weapon that is formed against you will prosper. (Isaiah 54:17 KJV)

But thanks be to God, which giveth us the victory through our Lord Jesus Christ. (1 Corinthians 15:57 KJV)

Fear thou not; for I am with thee: be not dismayed; for I am thy God: I will strengthen thee; yea, I will help thee; yea, I will uphold thee with the right hand of my righteousness. (Isaiah 41:10 KJV)

But thanks be to God, which giveth us the victory through our Lord Jesus Christ. (1 Corinthians 15:57 KJV)

Fear thou not; for I am with thee: be not dismayed; for I am thy God: I will strengthen thee; yea, I will help thee; yea, I will uphold thee with the right hand of my righteousness. (Isaiah 41:10 KJV)

These things I have spoken unto you, that in me ye might have peace. In the world ye shall have tribulation: but be of good cheer; I have overcome the world. (Proverbs 16:33 KJV)

Recognize the fear as a Satan attack and fight against it by taking authority over fear, subdue my thoughts by God promises. For God hath not given us the spirit of fear; but of power, and of love, and of a sound mind. (2 Timothy 1:7 KJV)

Wherefore take unto you the whole armour of God, that ye may be able to withstand in the evil day, and having done all, to stand. (Ephesians 6:13 KJV)

Submit yourselves therefore to God. Resist the devil, and he will flee from you. (James 4:7 KJV)

As I am privileged to be a child of God, I am allegeable through my special relationship with Him (as a child and parent) to apply all his promises to my life and condition. For as much then as the children are partakers of flesh and blood, he also himself likewise took part of the same; that through death he might destroy him that had the power of death, that is, the devil; And deliver them who through fear of death were all their lifetime subject to bondage. For verily he took not on him the nature of angels; but he took on him the seed of

Abraham. Wherefore in all things it behooved him to be made like unto his brethren, that he might be a merciful and faithful high priest in things pertaining to God, to make reconciliation for the sins of the people. (Hebrews 2:14–17 KJV)

What man is he that desireth life, and loveth many days, that he may see good? Keep thy tongue from evil, and thy lips from speaking guile. Depart from evil, and do good; seek peace, and pursue it. The eyes of the Lord are upon the righteous, and his ears are open unto their cry. (Psalm 34:12–15 KJV)

For I know the thoughts that I think toward you, saith the Lord, thoughts of peace, and not of evil, to give you an expected end. Then shall ye call upon me, and ye shall go and pray unto me, and I will hearken unto you. And ye shall seek me, and find me, when ye shall search for me with all your heart.

And I will be found of you, saith the Lord: and I will turn away your captivity. (Jeremiah 29:11–14 KJV)

Cast not away therefore your confidence, which hath great recompence of reward. (Hebrews 10:35 KJV)

The deadliest situation or condition is reversible with God. Nerveless what people is telling around or statistic or Internet when you try to find answer, everything is possible with God. What is possible—*everything.* That's it. No discussions. Behold, I am the

Lord, the God of all flesh; is anything too difficult for Me?" (Jeremiah 32:27 KJV)

Greater is he that is in you, than he that is in the world. (1 John 4:4 KJV)

Many are the afflictions of the righteous: but the Lord delivereth him out of them all. He keepeth all his bones: not one of them is broken. (Psalm 34:19–20 KJV)

And this is the confidence that we have in him, that, if we ask any thing according to his will, he heareth us: And if we know that he hear us, whatsoever we ask, we know that we have the petitions that we desired of him. (1 John 5:14–15 KJV)

And Jesus answering saith unto them, Have faith in God. For verily I say unto you, That whosoever shall say unto this mountain, Be thou removed, and be thou cast into the sea; and shall not doubt in his heart, but shall believe that those things which he saith shall come to pass; he shall have whatsoever he saith. Therefore, I say unto you, What things soever ye desire, when ye pray, believe that ye receive them, and ye shall have them. (Mark 11:22–23 KJV)

But if the Spirit of him that raised up Jesus from the dead dwell in you, he that raised up Christ from the dead shall also quicken your mortal bodies by his Spirit that dwelleth in you. (Romans 8:11 KJV)

Casting all your care upon him; for he careth for you. Be sober, be vigilant; because your adversary the devil, as a roaring lion, walketh about, seeking whom he may devour: Whom resist steadfast in the faith, knowing that the same afflictions are accomplished in your brethren that are in the world. But the God of all grace, who hath called us unto his eternal glory by Christ Jesus, after that ye have suffered a while, make you perfect, stablish, strengthen, settle you. (1 Peter 5:7–10 KJV)

Jesus said unto him, If thou canst believe, all things are possible to him that believeth. (Mark 9:23 KJV)

Is anything too hard for the Lord? (Genesis 18:14 KJV)

This I recall to my mind, therefore have I hope. It is of the Lord's mercies that we are not consumed, because his compassions fail not. They are new every morning: great is thy faithfulness. The Lord is my portion, saith my soul; therefore will I hope in him. (Lamentations 3:21–24 KJV)

The sorrows of death compassed me, and the pains of hell gat hold upon me: I found trouble and sorrow. Then called I upon the name of the Lord; O Lord, I beseech thee, deliver my soul. Gracious is the Lord, and righteous; yea, our God is merciful. The Lord preserveth the simple: I was brought low, and he helped me. Return unto thy rest, O my soul; for the Lord hath dealt bountifully with thee. For thou hast delivered my soul from death, mine eyes from tears, and my feet from falling. I will walk before the Lord in the land of the living. (Psalm 116:3–9 KJV)

I have seen his ways, and will heal him: I will lead him also, and restore comforts unto him and to his mourners. I create the fruit of the lips; Peace, peace to him that is far off, and to him that is near, saith the Lord; and I will heal him. (Isaiah 57:18 KJV)

Then shall thy light break forth as the morning, and thine health shall spring forth speedily: and thy righteousness shall go before thee; the glory of the Lord shall be thy rereward. (Isaiah 58:8 KJV)

I shall not die, but live, and declare the works of the Lord. (Psalm 118:17 KJV)

With long life will I satisfy him. (Psalm 91 KJV)

Behold, the Lord's hand is not shortened, that it cannot save; neither his ear heavy, that it cannot hear. (Isaiah 59:1 KJV)

Though a sinner do evil an hundred times, and his days be prolonged, yet surely I know that it shall be well with them that fear God, which fear before him. (Ecclesiastes 8:12 KJV)

In the way of righteousness is life: and in the pathway thereof there is no death. (Proverbs 12:28 KJV)

Surely he hath borne our griefs, and carried our sorrows: yet we did esteem him stricken, smitten of God, and afflicted. But he was wounded for our transgressions, he was bruised for our iniquities:

the chastisement of our peace was upon him; and with his stripes we are healed. (Isaiah 53:4–5 KJV)

And when the men of that place had knowledge of him, they sent out into all that country round about, and brought unto him all that were diseased; And besought him that they might only touch the hem of his garment: and as many as touched were made perfectly whole. (Matthew 14:34–35 KJV)

When thou passest through the waters, I will be with thee; and through the rivers, they shall not overflow thee: when thou walkest through the fire, thou shalt not be burned; neither shall the flame kindle upon thee. (Isaiah 43:2–3 KJV)

Now thanks be unto God, which always causeth us to triumph in Christ, and maketh manifest the savour of his knowledge by us in every place. (2 Corinthians 2:14 KJV)

CHAPTER 13

Medical Documents

Dear readers, I included this chapter in my book to prove that the story of *Fighting for Life* is real and has a happy end *only* because our God is real.

It doesn't matter how high your mountain is and how hot your fire. Where you are it is not the end because our God is the beginning and the end, and only He is holding tomorrow of your life.

My blessing and sincere wish is to stay healthy and keep peace not because of who you are but because of who He is.

I will be honored to help those who want to make a difference in their life. Make a step to prolong your health and longevity and reach your healthy goals with my holistic program. Please visit me and fill out the form for a free breakthrough initial consultation:

www.lubovhealthylongevity.com or
email: lubovhealthylongevity@gmail.com

From my Clinical History—First Diagnostic Result in Doha

CT ABDOMEN WITH CONTRAST OF 27.06.2013

There is a well-defined seven times 6 cm in diameter mass-like lesion with. Tiny calcific focus and showed patchy enhancement after intravenous contrast injection arising from the Left adrenal glands displacing. The left kidney downward and the limiting. The tail of the pancreas upward and also compressing on the medial aspect of the spleen but does not show any infiltration of the surrounding structure. There is about 2 cm in diameter rounded mass-like lesion present in the medial aspect of right breast. The liver spleen pancreas and lung parenchyma are normal.

Conclusion left adrenal mass with calcification most likely to be malignant in nature. Small mass present in the right breast and further investigation recommended for the breast.

Part of my Surgical Pathology Report:

Time Collected 03-Oct-2013 11:09
Time Reported 21-Oct-2013 11:05
Status Final
Time Received 03-Oct-2013 11:24
Time Transmitted 21-Oct-2013 11:06
Report Patient Name: Kulakova, Lyubov O
Specimen Description
Left adrenal gland, 7 myolipoma vs adrenocortical carcinoma
Diagnosis
Adrenal Gland (Left); Resection:

Oncocytic adrenal cortical carcinoma, 7,5 cm, 160g, vascular

Invasion present, tumor confined within adrenal gland, resection

Margin negative for malignancy (pT2).

Cross Description

Received is a single specimen container. The requisition and specimen container are labelled with the patient's name, Kulakova, Lyubov. The cassette and AP identifiers are labeled with the surgical Number SF13–23580.

202 g, 8,5 to 6,8 to 6,5 cm mass, encapsulated smooth border to adrenal tissue, cross-section of the mass adipose large vessels, hemorrhage and focal necrosis more than 5,. 20's. 160g. after fat is trimmed, mass measures 7,5 to 6,0 to 6,0 cm. MKO/ kid

The specimen is received fresh and is subsequently placed into formalin. The specimen container is labeled "left adrenal gland, 7 myolipoma vs adrenocortical carcinoma." The specimen consists of adrenal gland with attached adipose tissue. The specimen weighs 202 g. The fat is removed. The adrenal gland weighs 160g in the fresh state. The capsule is intact. The cut surfaces reveal a circumscribed tumor with measures 7,5 to 6,0 to 5,5 cm. The tumor has a thick fibrous capsule. The cut surfaces if the tumor are hemorrhagic tan with yellow flakes and areas of necrosis. The tumor appears to be confined within the adrenal gland and does not involve the resection margin. The surrounding adrenal gland appears unremarkable.

Sections:

The tumor and surrounding adrenal are submitted in A1 through A16 (vascular invasion in jA11/12).

Adipose tissue in A17. Additional sections other tumor are submitted in A18 – A23. MK/kid

MY JOURNEY TO HEALTH
STARTED FROM SICKNESS.

www.lubovhealthylongevity.com
email: lubovhealthylongevity@gmail.com

Lubov Oberemok (Kulakova) is the author of *Dancing in the Fire or Fighting for Life*, a board-certified holistic health practitioner, and the loving and caring mother of two. As a holistic health coach and nutritional consultant going through a midlife crisis, cancer, depression, anxiety, and insomnia, she made the decision to hold on to promises from God and keep her faith in Him. She found a unique way of healing, restoration, and physical and emotional rejuvenation with the union of spirit, mind, and soul.

Drawing on her knowledge and personal life path of faith in God fueled her passion to live an extraordinary life and to help clients and friends do the same, despite life's ups and downs. Reach your health goals naturally, in harmony with your inner self and your loved one. Be happy, look younger, and live longer. She will help you to create a personalized road map to health that suits your unique body, lifestyle, preferences, and goals. She will share her mastery in challenging clients to examine old patterns and beliefs that keep them stuck in a rut, identify meaningful goals, and design effective strategies to move ahead and create a healthy lifestyle.

Lubov graduated from the Institute for Integrative Nutrition (IIN) in New York and the Global College of Natural Medicine with Nutritional Consultant Program. She learned about detoxification, holistic healing, and more than one hundred dietary theories and studied a variety of practical lifestyle coaching methods. She is certified by the American Association of Drugless Practitioners and has a title of board-certified holistic health practitioner. She also holds her degree with distinction in library science from Europe.

Lubov delivers inspirational keynote speeches and gives workshops about life and health-changing transformation, constantly improving her education to fulfill the passion of spreading her message of faith: be happy, look younger, and live longer in balance and harmony of spirit, mind, and soul.

Printed in the United States
By Bookmasters